How to Become Famous

CRAFTED BY SKRIUWER

Copyright © 2024 by Skriuwer.

All rights reserved. No part of this book may be used or reproduced in any form whatsoever without written permission except in the case of brief quotations in critical articles or reviews.

For more information, contact : **kontakt@skriuwer.com** (www.skriuwer.com)

TABLE OF CONTENTS

CHAPTER 1: UNDERSTANDING FAME

- *Seeing the difference between fame and being well-liked*
- *Knowing the rewards and challenges of public attention*
- *Realizing that fame is not a fix for personal problems*

CHAPTER 2: FINDING YOUR STRENGTHS

- *Exploring hidden talents through practice and feedback*
- *Picking a skill or area that sparks true interest*
- *Listening to honest opinions from trusted sources*

CHAPTER 3: MAKING A CLEAR PLAN

- *Setting specific, workable goals for your progress*
- *Breaking down large goals into smaller steps*
- *Tracking results and adjusting your path as needed*

CHAPTER 4: BUILDING A PERSONAL IMAGE

- *Choosing a style or presentation that fits you*
- *Using online and offline platforms consistently*
- *Staying genuine while shaping how others see you*

CHAPTER 5: CONNECTING WITH PEOPLE

- *Finding the right places to meet peers and mentors*
- *Offering help and staying genuine in your relationships*
- *Following up politely and building long-term bonds*

CHAPTER 6: BUILDING SKILLS AND CONFIDENCE

- *Focusing on regular practice and self-improvement*
- *Seeking feedback from experts and mentors*
- *Handling mistakes without losing self-belief*

CHAPTER 7: STUDYING GOOD EXAMPLES

- *Observing top performers and extracting their methods*
- *Comparing different styles to find new ideas*
- *Avoiding blind imitation by keeping your own flavor*

CHAPTER 8: HANDLING PUBLIC ATTENTION

- *Staying calm when many people watch or criticize*
- *Maintaining boundaries to protect privacy*
- *Balancing the spotlight with personal well-being*

CHAPTER 9: DEALING WITH DOUBT

- *Recognizing triggers that spark uncertainty*
- *Turning self-criticism into motivation to improve*
- *Separating harmful doubt from helpful caution*

CHAPTER 10: SHARING YOUR STORY ONLINE

- *Choosing the right platforms for your talent*
- *Blending skill showcases with personal insights*
- *Staying authentic in a crowded digital space*

CHAPTER 11: USING TRADITIONAL MEDIA

- Approaching newspapers, radio, and TV outlets politely
- Making a simple press release or media kit
- Being prepared for interviews and local features

CHAPTER 12: REACHING THE RIGHT AUDIENCE

- Identifying who benefits most from your work
- Tailoring your messaging to audience preferences
- Avoiding wasted efforts on uninterested groups

CHAPTER 13: BUILDING A STRONG MINDSET

- Embracing challenges and setbacks as growth steps
- Turning negative thoughts into action plans
- Practicing habits that boost mental toughness

CHAPTER 14: HANDLING STRESS

- Recognizing early signs of overload
- Using healthy routines to calm body and mind
- Balancing work demands with personal rest

CHAPTER 15: AVOIDING MISTAKES

- Preventing careless errors through planning and checks
- Listening to warnings or feedback from mentors
- Treating others respectfully to protect your image

CHAPTER 16: ADJUSTING TO NEW SITUATIONS

- *Reading the room in unfamiliar or bigger venues*
- *Blending your core style with fresh expectations*
- *Accepting collaboration while safeguarding personal identity*

CHAPTER 17: STAYING UNIQUE

- *Highlighting the special traits that set you apart*
- *Avoiding empty gimmicks and building real style*
- *Standing up for your creative identity over trends*

CHAPTER 18: BALANCING WORK AND HOME

- *Maintaining relationships alongside a busy schedule*
- *Delegating tasks and setting clear boundaries*
- *Preserving health and personal downtime for stability*

CHAPTER 19: USING FEEDBACK WELL

- *Filtering out mean attacks versus helpful critiques*
- *Using constructive comments to refine your craft*
- *Staying confident without ignoring repeated advice*

CHAPTER 20: STAYING TRUE TO YOUR BELIEFS

- *Identifying core values and holding to them under pressure*
- *Politely declining offers that violate your ethics*
- *Preserving integrity in both public and private life*

CHAPTER 1: UNDERSTANDING FAME

Fame is when many people know who you are and talk about you. This can happen if you do something special, if you stand out in your field, or if you appear on many channels where people can see or hear you. People who are famous can be movie stars, musicians, athletes, writers, or even people who share videos online. Sometimes, a person can also become famous because of a single event, like inventing something very useful or achieving a record that no one else has reached. Fame can look exciting from the outside, but there is much more to it than bright lights and happy faces.

It is important to know that fame is not the same as being well-liked. Some famous people are liked and admired, and some are well-known for less positive reasons. So, when we talk about fame in this book, we are looking at how to be widely recognized for your talents and efforts, rather than for unkind or harmful acts. If you aim to be famous for good reasons, you usually have a goal that helps others or entertains them in some way. For example, you could be famous for singing songs that lift people's moods, writing funny stories that bring smiles, or making art that inspires others.

Fame can come in different forms. Some people are famous in a small area, like a neighborhood or town, while others are known around the world. For example, a local teacher can be famous among students and parents for being the best teacher in the area, but that same teacher may not be known in another city. Meanwhile, a movie star can be famous in many different countries, because their face is shown in films or on television. It is also possible to be famous on the internet through video channels or social media pages. In these spaces, a person can gather followers from all parts of the world.

There are many reasons why people aim for fame. Some wish for money, because famous people can sometimes earn more for their work. Some want to influence the world and share their ideas with others. If you are a scientist who finds a new way to help the environment, you could use your fame to spread your message. If you are an athlete who excels in a sport, you might use your fame to inspire children to stay healthy and active. So, fame can be a tool that allows you to spread your voice and ideas further than you could on your own.

At the same time, there are costs that come with fame. One of the biggest costs is the loss of privacy. When many people know your name and face, they might stop you on the street, ask for pictures, or talk about your life even if they do not know you personally. For some, this feels overwhelming. They cannot do simple tasks in public without being watched or followed. Another problem could be the pressure to always act in a certain way so that you do not upset your supporters. Some people may even make rumors about you if they do not like how you behave. This can feel stressful and lonely at times.

Another thing to consider is that fame does not always last. You might be well-known for a period, and then, as people find new faces and new stories, they might forget about you. Some people find it hard to handle this shift, because they get used to the attention and applause, then suddenly fewer people recognize them. This can lead to sadness or confusion. So, before you step into a path toward being famous, it is wise to understand that it might not be permanent.

There are also differences between earning fame through real skill and gaining it by accident. People who work on their talent for a long time often have a lasting impact. They might be an actor who trains in many roles or a writer who keeps writing new stories. Meanwhile, someone might get famous overnight for doing something that goes viral on the internet. This can happen very fast, but it also might fade fast. This does not mean one type of fame is always better than the other, but if you aim for a long, steady path, you might want to focus on something you can keep doing over time, like playing a sport at a high level or working on music that grows in quality with each performance.

It is also important to see that fame can affect your friendships and family life. Some people start to feel that they have to work more and more, accepting every chance to be seen, which might cause them to spend less time with their loved ones. Others might face jealousy or false gossip if those around them are not supportive. When you become famous, some people will like you more, and others might dislike you without real cause. Not everyone will be happy for you. You might hear unkind comments on the internet or read mean opinions about yourself. Handling that can be difficult, especially if you read hurtful things every day.

Fame has changed over time. Many years ago, you often had to be in movies, on TV, or in a big newspaper to be widely recognized. Now, the internet gives more people a chance to be seen. You could post a funny video or a creative piece of artwork and get shared by millions. This can open doors that once were only open to those who had big movie deals or record contracts. On the other hand, this also means it is easier for many people to try to become famous at once. The online world can feel crowded, and standing out might not be simple.

Another point to understand is that being well-known does not always mean you are doing something good for yourself. Some people chase fame because they think it will fix their problems or make them happy. They may believe that if everyone knows them, they will no longer feel lonely or sad. But that is not always true. Famous people can still feel lonely, and the attention can even make them more stressed. Happiness and comfort often come from a strong sense of who you are and from having genuine friends and family. Fame is not a magic trick that solves all problems.

It might help you to watch or read interviews with people who have experienced fame. They often share that it can be both nice and tiring. They might enjoy the support and love from fans, but they also might miss having an ordinary life. Some say they wish they could go to the grocery store or a park without being noticed. Others talk about how they have to be careful about who they trust, because sometimes people try to use them for money or status. Hearing these stories can help you decide if you truly want to go down this road.

You might ask, "If fame can be so hard, why do people still chase it?" There are many answers. For one, it can feel good to have others enjoy your work. If you are a singer, you might like it when thousands of people sing your song. If you are a teacher, you might like being honored for your teaching. Also, with fame, you might get new chances to do things you love. A known chef might open more restaurants, a known writer might get better deals for book releases, and a known actor might get more roles. So, there are rewards that come with recognition. It is just important to know that there is more to it than the bright side.

In the modern world, fame can come from many places. Some people get recognized by being on reality shows, others start streaming themselves playing video games, and some gain attention by sharing their art on social media. There is no single way to do it. At the same time, there is competition in nearly every field. So, if you want to stand out, you need to think about what you have to offer that is different. You cannot simply copy someone else's style and expect to become the next big name. You need your own approach.

Some people also like the idea of being a role model. When you are in the public eye, younger people might look up to you. They might see you as proof that they can also achieve something. This can be a good reason to aim for fame. It can push you to work harder and be a good example. However, it can be a big responsibility, because if you make a mistake, many eyes are on you and might point it out. Everybody makes mistakes, but when you are well-known, those mistakes can spread fast in the news or on social media.

Fame might also come with more money, but this is not always guaranteed. Some actors in small movies might be famous in some circles but not very rich. Some online creators might have a lot of fans, but they still have to struggle with normal expenses. So, if your main reason for seeking fame is wealth, you should be careful. It might not work the way you think. A better reason to aim for recognition is that you truly like what you do and want to share it with as many people as possible.

Another question that is common: "Is fame only for outgoing people?" The answer is no. You can be an introvert and still be recognized for your work. For instance, some best-selling writers are quiet in public but have strong ideas that people love. Some scientists become well-known for big discoveries but prefer a calm life outside the lab. Fame does not look the same for everyone. What matters is whether you do something that people find interesting or meaningful.

So, to sum up this chapter, understanding fame is about seeing both the good and the not-so-good sides. It is about knowing that fame can let you share your skills and ideas with more people, but it can also bring stress, less privacy, and a sense of pressure. Before seeking it, you should decide if it fits your goals. If you think it does, then you can read on to learn how to prepare for it step by step. If you are not sure, it is still a good idea to understand these aspects, because sometimes fame finds people who are not even looking for it, and it helps to be ready.

Remember, fame is not all that matters. You can have a happy and successful life without being famous. The choice is personal. If you do want to be widely recognized, then learning about fame, planning carefully, and staying true to who you are can make the process safer and more rewarding. Let's now look at the first concrete step in this process: finding what you are good at. That is the key to choosing a clear path and giving yourself the best chance for genuine success.

CHAPTER 2: FINDING YOUR STRENGTHS

Finding your strengths is a key step if you want to be famous. Many famous people are known for one or two strong points, like singing, acting, playing a sport, or writing. Others are recognized for their knowledge in science, or for a special skill that helps people in some way. Fame often grows when you have something unique that draws attention or gives value to people. This can be entertainment, education, or support. But before any of that, you need to figure out what you are naturally good at, or what you can get good at with practice.

You might wonder how to find your strengths. One simple method is to try different activities. You do not have to be amazing right away. Instead, pay attention to activities that make you feel interested and focused. For example, if you try dancing and notice that you have a good sense of rhythm and feel excited to learn new steps, that might be a clue that dancing could be a strength. Or if you like to draw and others say your pictures look creative, that could be a sign that art is one of your strong points.

Asking for feedback from friends and family can also help. Sometimes, they can see talents in you that you might miss. For instance, maybe you are great at making people laugh, and others say you have a real gift for telling jokes or stories. That might be a clue you could do well in comedy or acting. On the other hand, if people often tell you that you give good advice, maybe you have strong communication skills that can be useful in broadcasting or public speaking. Listening to people you trust can guide you toward talents that you might not notice on your own.

You can also pay attention to the activities that feel easy for you, even if they are hard for others. If you pick up a guitar and find chords simple to remember, that might mean you have a musical gift. If you learn languages fast, that might be another strong point. However, just because something feels easy does not mean it is your only path. Sometimes, our real strengths are things we care about, but we still need to practice a lot before we see true success. It can be a mix of natural ability and strong motivation.

When you are trying to find your strengths, it can help to make a list of the things you enjoy. Write down everything that you like doing, whether it is painting, playing video games, solving math problems, or singing. Then, mark which ones you think you do better than most of your friends or classmates. You do not have to be the best in the world. You just need to see if you stand out in your area. If you find a few items on your list that feel both fun and somewhat easy, keep those in mind as possible areas for growth.

Some people feel worried if they cannot find any talent right away. They might think, "I am not great at anything." But remember that talents can be hidden, and you might just need time and practice to uncover them. For example, maybe you never tried acting, so you do not know if you would be good at it. Or maybe you never tried to write short stories, so you do not know if you have a knack for words. That is why exploring new activities can be so helpful. You never know which one might bring out your hidden strengths.

Finding your strengths is also about knowing what you like. If you feel bored by an activity, even if you are good at it, you might not want to spend years doing it. Fame often requires you to keep working on the same skill for a long time, so it helps if you really care about that skill. For instance, if you are good at sports but do not love the hard practice, you might not go far in that area. But if you love drawing so much that you stay up late sketching, that love can push you to become great at it.

Another way to find strengths is to see where you have improved a lot. For example, think about subjects in school. Maybe you were average in math at first, but then you started putting in extra time, and now you are one of the top students in your class. That might show that you are good at focusing when a topic catches your eye. Or, if you joined a singing group and found your voice getting stronger each month, that could mean you have a gift for singing that grows when you put in effort.

It can also help to look at famous people you admire. Notice what they are known for and compare that to your own interests. Do not copy them exactly. Instead, use them as an example to see how they built their success on top of their talents. If you look up to a famous soccer player because they are fast and clever, see if you share a love of soccer. If you do, you can practice in a way that brings out your best qualities. If you admire a famous writer for their books, see if you have fun creating stories, too.

Once you have some idea of your strengths, it is helpful to narrow them down. You might have many interests, but if you try to be famous for all of them at once, it can lead to confusion. It might be wiser to pick one or two main areas that you care about deeply. If you see that you are good at writing stories and also at painting pictures, you could focus on both if they fit together, or choose one if you want to give it all your attention. This focus helps you get better in a clearer way, which can help you stand out.

Think of each strength as a seed that you can make better with consistent work. If you pick too many seeds to handle at once, you might not see real results in any of them. But if you pick one seed and give it enough time and energy, you might reach a high level. Try to look at your favorite activities and ask yourself which one you want to spend hours practicing. Which one makes you excited about learning new information or trying new methods? That feeling is a big clue that it is the right area for you.

It is also helpful to be honest about your weaknesses. If you find that you cannot carry a tune, maybe singing is not your best path. If you get exhausted playing sports, maybe that is not right for you. That does not mean you can never do these activities for fun. You just might not want to aim for fame in that particular field. Instead, use your energy where you have a better chance to shine. People who stand out in their areas often know what they are good at and where they struggle, so they can place their focus wisely.

Another important aspect is to test your strengths in real-world situations. For example, if you think you are good at giving speeches, try giving one in class or to a small group. See how they respond. Do they look interested? Do they tell you they learned something new or felt inspired? If you get a strong positive reaction, that might be a signal that you have a real strength in public speaking. If you think you are good at writing stories, share them with a few people or even a local writing club. Check if they say your stories are engaging. You might even try entering small contests to see if your work stands out.

At the same time, do not be discouraged by failure. Sometimes, you might give a speech or write a story, and people might not like it at first. That does not always mean you lack skill. It could mean you need to practice more or try a different style. However, if you see that you keep trying and keep feeling miserable about it, then maybe it is not the right field. On the other hand, if you see that each time you try, you get a bit better and feel motivated, that is a good sign.

Keep in mind that finding your strengths is not about being perfect. You might see that you are good at playing guitar but not at singing. That is okay. You can still focus on becoming a great guitar player who works with a singer. Or, if you love telling jokes but not performing on stage, you could write jokes for others to perform. Think of ways you can use what you have, rather than forcing yourself to do something that feels uncomfortable and unnatural.

In some cases, you can pair two strengths to create a fresh approach. For example, if you are good at cooking and also at talking in front of a camera, maybe you can share cooking videos online. If you are good at playing an instrument and also good at writing, you could write songs that you perform. Combining two or more strengths can help you stand out from others who might only focus on one. The key is to pick activities that fit well together and make you happy.

Another tip is to think about what you did when you were younger. Sometimes, children show early signs of their strengths by wanting to do certain activities again and again. Maybe you always drew pictures, or always told funny stories to friends. These early hints can guide you now if you forgot what you once loved. You can think, "When I was small, I spent hours building things with blocks. Maybe I have a talent for design or engineering." Reflecting on these early interests might reignite a passion you did not realize you had.

You should also be patient as you find your strengths. Some people know right away what they love. Others take longer. It is not a race. It is more important that you really understand what you are good at than to decide right away. If you rush, you might pick an area that does not truly fit, and you could waste time. If you allow yourself to explore, you might discover a skill that amazes you. So, do not worry if it takes months or even years to feel certain about your strong points.

Once you feel that you have found one or two strengths, you can begin to think about how these might lead to recognition. Fame often grows when people see consistent proof of your skill. If you are a writer, that means writing many pieces and sharing them. If you are a singer, that means practicing your voice and performing whenever you can. But remember, you do not have to rush into seeking attention immediately. First, focus on getting better and more comfortable with your chosen activity. After that, you can think about ways to share it with the public.

It is also worth noting that strengths can change or expand. You might start in one area and later move to another. Some famous actors started as musicians, and some writers started as painters. Life can shift, and you can grow in new ways. But having at least one clear skill at first can help you stand out. It gives people a reason to remember you. Then, if you want to add other skills later, you can. The important thing is to start by knowing yourself as you are now.

In closing, finding your strengths is like opening a door. Once you know what you are good at and what you enjoy, you can step forward with more confidence. You will have a better idea of what to practice and how to use your energy. You will also feel more sure about the direction to take. In the next chapters, we will talk about planning and other practical steps that can help you move closer to being recognized. But no matter how many tips you get, your own strengths and interests are what will set you apart. So, spend time exploring, listen to honest feedback, and trust your instincts. If you truly enjoy something and people notice your talent in that area, that is a strong hint you are on the right track.

CHAPTER 3: MAKING A CLEAR PLAN

Having a plan is helpful if you want to become famous. Even if you have great talents, you still need a path that shows you what to do next. This helps you move forward without feeling lost. A plan can include small goals, daily tasks, and long-term aims. It can also help you measure your progress. When you see each step clearly, you are more likely to keep going, even if things get hard. In this chapter, we will look at ways to build a good plan that fits your strengths and your personal goals.

---

1. **Why a Plan Matters**

Imagine you are trying to climb a tall mountain. If you look at the top and feel confused about which way to go, you might not even begin. But if you have a map with marked paths, you know where to place your feet next. In the same way, a plan to become famous gives you directions. It tells you when to practice, how to show your work to others, and how to keep track of your growth. Without a plan, you might get stuck or spend your time on unhelpful tasks that do not bring you closer to the recognition you want.

A plan also helps you use your time wisely. Time is important because you only have a certain number of hours each day. If you decide how to spend those hours in a careful way, you can make steady progress. For example, if you want to become a famous singer, you might plan to practice singing for one hour, do vocal exercises for another hour, and then post a short recording on a website where people can hear your voice. That routine, done often, can bring you closer to your dream than random actions would.

---

2. **Setting Clear Goals**

A plan begins with goals. These goals should be specific. For instance, saying "I want to be famous" is not detailed enough. Instead, you might say, "I want to gain 10,000 online followers who enjoy my comedy videos," or "I want to perform in front of 500 people at a local event next year." A specific goal helps you see exactly what you need to do. It also helps you know when you have reached your target.

Try to set goals that feel possible but also make you work hard. If you set a goal that is too easy, you might not grow. If you set one that is impossible right now, you might get discouraged and quit. You can start with smaller goals, such as writing one new song each week if you are a songwriter, or practicing an hour of dance each day if you want to be a dancer. These smaller goals can then lead to bigger goals, like performing on a bigger stage or getting 100,000 fans online.

---

3. **Breaking Down Large Goals**

Sometimes, big goals seem scary or overwhelming. For example, if you want to write a book, you may feel you need to write hundreds of pages. Instead of thinking, "I need to write hundreds of pages," break that into smaller steps. Say, "I will write two pages per day." If you keep doing that, those pages will add up. The same idea applies to any path toward fame. If you want to become well-known for art, you might break it down into steps like:

- Sketching each day
- Finishing one large piece each month
- Sharing your artwork online or in local shows
- Connecting with other artists in the community

By focusing on small tasks, you make steady progress without feeling too much pressure. Each completed step is a little success. Over time, these small successes can build into something much bigger.

---

4. **Creating a Timeline**

A timeline is a schedule of when you want to complete each task. It can be as simple as deciding that you will reach your smaller goal in one month, then your bigger goal in six months, and then an even bigger one in a year. This timeline is not meant to lock you in. It is more like a guide that helps you see if you are moving too slowly or too quickly.

For example, if you plan to do small performances every month for a year, that is a simple timeline. After six months, you can check if you have done six performances. If you have not, you might see why. Maybe you need to look for more open events. Maybe you need to contact more organizers. This keeps you honest with yourself about your efforts.

5. **Planning Your Resources**

You might need certain things to reach your goals. This could be tools (like a camera for filming, a microphone for singing, or equipment for sports) or money for lessons or travel. Make a list of what you need and how you will get it. For instance, if you need a better camera, plan how you will save money or earn it. If you need singing lessons, find someone who teaches them at a cost you can manage. By planning your resources ahead of time, you avoid surprises. You also make sure that you are prepared to move forward as soon as the time is right.

You may also need people to help you. This can include a coach, a teacher, or friends who support you. Think about who can assist you, and include them in your plan. For instance, if your friend has a camera and is willing to film your performances, add that to your plan. If a teacher can guide your skill development, set a schedule for lessons. These steps can make the path much smoother.

6. **Practicing Consistently**

No plan works without consistent practice. If your strength is singing, you should make daily or weekly practice a key part of your plan. If your strength is writing, plan to write at specific times. Consistency is what helps you become truly good at what you do. When you practice often, you grow not just in skill but also in confidence.

An easy way to stay consistent is to use a calendar or a planner. Write down the times when you will practice. Even if you do not feel like practicing on some days, do it anyway, if possible. That is how progress happens. Over time, the repeated practice will pay off, and you will see clear improvement.

7. **Staying Flexible**

A plan is not carved in stone. Life changes, and sometimes your plan has to change too. You might face challenges that you did not expect. You might get a chance to do something special that was not in your original plan. Staying flexible means you can adjust your timeline and goals as needed.

For instance, maybe you planned to post one video a week, but you get an offer to do a live show somewhere. You might decide to skip posting a video that week so you can prepare for the show. That does not mean your plan failed. It just means you are making a smart choice to use a new chance in the best way. The important thing is not to quit your plan forever but to adapt it so it still serves you well.

8. **Measuring Your Progress**

It helps to keep track of how far you have come. This can be done in many ways. You can mark on a chart each time you do a task. You can record your performances and compare them over time. You can track the number of followers or fans you have and note how that number changes month by month. By keeping track, you see patterns. If you notice you are not growing as quickly as you hoped, you can look at what might be going wrong. Maybe you need more practice, or maybe you need to share your work in a different place.

Measuring progress also helps you see that you have improved, which can motivate you. Sometimes, you might feel like nothing is happening, but when you look back at a chart or at old videos, you might realize that your singing has gotten much better or your drawings are more detailed. This can give you a push to keep going.

9. **Setting Milestones for Public Exposure**

Part of becoming famous is letting people see what you do. This might mean performing at events, showing your work online, or being part of contests. Include these in your plan as well. For example, you might set a milestone to perform at a local event within three months, then at a bigger event in six months, and so on. You might plan to upload a certain number of videos or blog posts to build a presence online. You do not have to be everywhere at once. Instead, choose one or two platforms or venues that make sense for your skill, and plan how often you will appear there.

10. **Reviewing and Adjusting**

After a few weeks or months, take time to review how your plan is going. Ask yourself:

- Have I reached the small goals I set?
- Am I making progress in my skill?
- Did I find new ideas or people to help me?
- Do I still feel motivated by my goals?

If you see that something is off track, make changes. If you are reaching your goals too easily, try bigger goals. If your goals feel impossible, break them into smaller steps or extend the timeline. The plan should serve you, not stress you out to a point where you want to quit. Adjusting is a normal part of any big attempt, including the path to fame.

11. **Balancing Planning with Action**

While making a plan is key, there can be a problem if you spend too much time planning and not enough time doing. You should not get stuck in planning mode. Write down the key parts, then start acting on them. If you want to improve your art, you must draw or paint regularly. If you want to improve your guitar playing, you must play the guitar often. No plan will work unless you take real steps. The purpose of the plan is to guide those steps, not to replace them.

12. **Getting Advice from Mentors**

If you know someone who is successful in your field, try asking them for guidance. They might give you ideas for your plan that you never thought of. They can also warn you about mistakes to avoid. Mentors can be teachers, older friends, or professionals who agree to help you. You can share your plan with them and see what they say. Even if they only give you a few tips, those tips might save you a lot of trouble later.

Be polite when you reach out to potential mentors. They might be busy. Ask short, clear questions. Show that you respect their time. Even if they cannot help much, you will learn from the experience. If you do find someone who is willing to guide you, keep in touch and update them on your progress. They might continue to give you ideas as you move along.

13. **Staying Motivated**

Even with a plan, you might have days when you feel tired or discouraged. That is normal. One way to stay motivated is to look at your plan and see how far you have come. If you wrote it down, review the tasks you already finished. Remind yourself why you started in the first place. Maybe you want to share your gift of music with the world, or you want to bring smiles through your comedy. Thinking about that purpose can give you energy to keep moving.

Another idea is to reward yourself when you reach a goal. This does not have to be a big prize. It could be allowing yourself a fun activity or a relaxing break. But be careful to keep your focus on the main reason for your plan, which is to build your skill and become known for it. If rewards help you stay on track, that is good. Just remember not to let them distract you from the work you need to do.

14. **Handling Distractions**

When you have a plan, you might notice that certain things distract you from your tasks. It could be spending too many hours on social media, playing games, or watching TV. While breaks are healthy, too much time on unhelpful things can slow your progress. If you see that something is taking away from your practice time, try to limit it. For instance, you might decide you will only watch one episode of your favorite show after finishing your daily tasks. Finding the right balance between work and rest is an important part of staying on track.

15. **Planning for Challenges**

You can guess that things will not always go smoothly. There might be times when you cannot practice because you are sick or busy. You might find that some people do not like your work. You might post a video and get a small number of views. Instead of letting these challenges discourage you, plan for them. Tell yourself, "I know there will be tough moments. When they happen, I will take a step back, see what went wrong, and try again." Knowing that challenges will come can make them feel less surprising. Also, having a plan for how to handle them keeps you from giving up too easily.

---

16. **Keeping Your Plan Simple**

A good plan does not have to be too fancy. It can be a page with your main goal at the top, a list of smaller goals, and a rough timeline. You can keep it on your wall or in a notebook. As long as it is clear and you can follow it, that is enough. If you like technology, you can use an app to track your tasks. But do not make it so complicated that you spend more time updating your plan than working on your skill. Simplicity helps you focus on what matters: building your talent and sharing it.

---

17. **Confidence and Belief in Your Plan**

If you do not believe in your plan, you will not follow it. You have to trust that each small task has a purpose. For example, if you have scheduled 30 minutes every morning to practice the piano, believe that those 30 minutes will add up over weeks and months. That belief can keep you consistent. If you doubt that your practice is helping, you might lose interest. So, remind yourself of why you set up the plan the way you did. Focus on the results you want to see in the future.

Sometimes, it helps to look at stories of people who became successful in your field. Often, they mention that they practiced or worked every day for years before people noticed them. This can give you faith that your small steps matter. It also shows you that big achievements rarely happen instantly.

18. Being Realistic About Time and Effort

When you make a plan, it is easy to overestimate or underestimate how long things take. You might think you can master a skill in a few weeks, only to find you need months or years. Be honest with yourself about how long it can take to become truly skilled. Being famous usually does not happen overnight. Even people who seem to "appear out of nowhere" often practiced quietly for a long time before they were discovered.

By being honest, you reduce the risk of disappointment. If you tell yourself, "I will learn basic guitar chords in three months," that might be more realistic than saying "I will become a guitar star in three months." Realistic goals help you keep a healthy mindset. They also allow you to see genuine growth as you move forward step by step.

19. Learning from Setbacks

Setbacks are moments when you feel like you moved backwards or hit a wall. Maybe you signed up for a local show and nobody came to watch, or you posted a video that got negative comments. These moments can hurt, but they are also chances to learn. Ask yourself what went wrong. Did you pick a bad time for the show? Did you share your video with the wrong audience? Did you ignore certain parts of your skill that need more work? By looking at the root of the problem, you can adjust your plan.

One key is not to see setbacks as final. They are normal bumps in the road. If you treat them as lessons, you will come out stronger and smarter. If you give up at every setback, you will never move forward. Adjust your plan, try something different, or seek advice, and keep going.

20. Putting It All Together

Making a clear plan involves:

1. Setting specific goals that push you but are possible.

2. Breaking those goals into smaller tasks.
3. Creating a timeline for when you will finish those tasks.
4. Planning resources, lessons, and help from others.
5. Practicing consistently and staying flexible.
6. Measuring progress to stay motivated.
7. Taking action and reviewing your plan often.
8. Learning from setbacks and adjusting as needed.

When you have these steps in place, you are not wandering aimlessly. You know what you want, and you have a roadmap to reach it. You will still need to work hard, and it may take time, but a solid plan makes a real difference. It helps you focus on what matters most—improving your skill and getting your name out there.

In the end, your plan is your personal guide. It is not something you show off to others necessarily. It is a tool for you to stay on the right track. If you follow it with discipline, you will likely see progress that could lead to the fame you seek. Keep in mind that the plan might change as you learn new things or grow in unexpected ways. That is fine. The important part is that you keep moving in a way that makes sense for your talents, your goals, and your well-being.

CHAPTER 4: BUILDING A PERSONAL IMAGE

A personal image is how the world sees you. It includes your appearance, your actions, your words, and the overall feeling people get when they think of you. If you are aiming to be famous, you need to think about how you present yourself. This does not mean changing who you are deep inside. Instead, it means deciding how you want your strengths and personality to show up for others. In this chapter, we will talk about why a personal image matters, how to shape it in an honest way, and how to keep it consistent as you grow in recognition.

1. **Why Personal Image Matters**

When people hear your name or see your face, they form opinions very quickly. They might think you are friendly, serious, creative, funny, or something else, based on what they see or hear. Your personal image helps guide those first impressions. A strong and clear image can draw people to you, help them remember you, and make them more likely to pay attention to your work.

For example, if you want to be known as a singer who shares uplifting songs, you might dress in a bright style, use colors or patterns in your videos, and talk in a friendly tone. When people see or hear you, they pick up on that feeling. Your personal image becomes part of your identity, and when people see it, they immediately think of your music and message.

2. **Deciding What You Want to Show**

Before building your image, think about what you want to express to others. Are you a relaxed person who wants to bring calm feelings to your audience? Do you want to be seen as a serious athlete who focuses on hard work and discipline? Or maybe you want people to see you as playful and imaginative, especially if you do comedy or children's entertainment. Pick a few key traits that fit you naturally. You do not have to force anything that feels fake. The idea is to highlight qualities that are already part of your personality and talents.

It can be useful to list these qualities. For example:

- Friendly
- Energetic
- Creative
- Helpful

These words can guide decisions about how you dress, how you speak to people, and what kind of content you share online. If you pick "friendly" and "creative" as your main qualities, you might choose bright outfits and post behind-the-scenes looks at your artistic process, letting people feel close to you.

---

3. **Being True to Yourself**

A personal image should be honest, or you might feel uncomfortable. Some people think they need to put on a fake persona to get attention. That can work for a short time, but it often feels tiring and can lead to confusion. For instance, if you pretend to be very confident when you do not feel that way, you might slip up when you are tired or stressed. Then people might think you are hiding something. It is usually better to be a version of yourself that is just a bit more polished or focused, rather than something that is completely invented.

Being true to yourself also means acknowledging your own style. If you are naturally quiet, you can still have a strong image by showing depth and thoughtfulness. If you are loud and playful, you can show that in a fun way. People appreciate realness because it stands out in a world where many things feel staged. When they sense that you are genuine, they are more likely to connect with you and stay interested in what you do.

---

4. **Choosing a Look**

Your look is part of your personal image. It includes clothes, hairstyle, makeup (if you wear it), and any accessories. You do not have to dress in a certain way just because others do. Instead, think about what matches your chosen qualities. If your focus is sports, you might appear more often in athletic clothes. If you are a visual artist, you might wear outfits that show color or pattern, reflecting your creative mind.

Try to be consistent. If you choose a certain style that is easy for you to keep, that will help people remember you. This does not mean you can never change. Over time, you might refresh your style. But if you change it too often or too drastically, it can confuse people. They might not be sure who you are trying to be. So, pick a look that feels right and aligns with how you want to be seen. Something that still feels comfortable for you is key, because if you feel awkward, it might show.

5. **Speaking and Acting**

Words and actions also shape your personal image. If you choose to be friendly and helpful, that should show in the way you speak to interviewers, fans, or anyone you meet. You might smile often, use a warm tone, and offer kind words. On the other hand, if you want to be seen as intense and focused (for example, in a competitive field like sports or gaming), you might speak more directly and use shorter answers. The point is not to be rude, but to match the style you are aiming for.

Your actions matter too. If you want to be known as a caring person who values honesty, make sure your behavior matches that. Avoid doing things that clash with your stated values. If people catch you acting in ways that do not line up with your image, they might lose trust. This is especially important in the age of social media, where videos and pictures can spread fast.

6. **Online Presence**

These days, your online presence is a big part of your personal image. Whether you are on a video platform, a social network, or a photo-sharing app, how you present yourself can shape how people see you. Use your main qualities as a guide for what you post. If you are trying to be seen as creative, share artwork, behind-the-scenes glimpses of your process, and stories about what inspires you. If you want to appear professional, keep your posts focused on your achievements, advice, or clear examples of your skill.

It is important to stay consistent across different platforms. If you post funny, lighthearted content on one page but very serious, formal content on another, people might get confused about who you really are. That does not mean you can only share one type of post. You can show different sides of your personality. But keep the overall tone in line with your chosen qualities. Also, be mindful of what you say in comments or private messages because even those can be shared publicly if someone decides to take a screenshot. Your words can follow you for a long time, so think before you type.

---

7. **Creating a Simple Message**

Some famous people have a short phrase or idea that sums up who they are or what they do. This is sometimes called a tagline or slogan. It can be a helpful tool to make your image stick in people's minds. For example, if you are a dancer, you might have a phrase like "Dance is my way to spread joy." This quick statement can guide your actions and remind people what you stand for. Keep it simple and real.

You do not have to use this slogan everywhere, but you can put it in your social media profiles, on your website (if you have one), or even say it in interviews. It gives people something easy to remember about you. The more they see or hear this phrase, the more it becomes linked to you in their minds.

---

8. **Avoiding Controversy If Possible**

While some people gain attention by being controversial, it can hurt your long-term image unless you truly want to be known for stirring up strong emotions. If your personal image is about creativity and kindness, getting involved in heated arguments or posting negative comments online might damage that image. Be cautious about expressing strong opinions on subjects that could offend your audience unless it is very important to you.

Sometimes, you might have strong views on real issues. That is okay, and showing your real self can build trust with some people. But be mindful of how and where you share these views. Think about the effect on your reputation. If you do want to take a stand on something, be ready for mixed reactions. Some will support you, and others might push back.

9. **Protecting Your Private Side**

Being famous often means that strangers have opinions about your life. This can feel like pressure. One way to manage that is to decide which parts of your life you will keep private. You do not have to share every detail about your family, your home, or your personal struggles. In fact, having some privacy can help you stay sane as your public image grows.

Think about what you are willing to discuss and what you would rather keep to yourself. For example, you might choose to share stories about your practice routine but keep your personal relationships private. If people ask you personal questions, it is fine to say you prefer not to talk about that topic. Just do it politely. By setting these boundaries, you can keep a sense of control over your life.

10. **Staying Consistent Over Time**

A personal image should not change too randomly. Once people get an idea of who you are, frequent changes can confuse them. That does not mean you can never evolve. Everyone grows and learns new things as they move forward. But you might want to shift your image step by step. For example, if you started out as a playful comedian and later want to be seen as a serious actor, you can gradually introduce roles or material that show your serious side. Do it in a way that feels natural, so your fans have time to adjust.

11. **Handling Criticism About Your Image**

When you are in the public eye, some people might make fun of your style or think you are pretending. That can be painful, especially if you have worked hard to create an honest image. Try not to let it discourage you. If the criticism is rude and without reason, it might be best to ignore it. If it is polite and points out something that might be harming your image, you could think about whether there is some truth to it.

For example, someone might say, "Your style comes across as too flashy for someone who says they want to be serious." If that rings true, you can adjust. If it does not make sense to you, let it go. Not everyone will like you, no matter what image you create. Focus on connecting with those who appreciate your work and your attitude.

---

12. Building Trust Through Honesty

Trust is a powerful thing when building a personal image. If people believe that you mean what you say and do what you promise, they are more likely to become loyal fans. One way to build trust is by being transparent about your process and your thoughts, within reason. For example, if you are a singer, you can show short clips of your vocal training. If you are a writer, you can share glimpses of your writing process. This openness helps people feel close to you.

However, honesty also means admitting mistakes. If you ever mess up or do something people do not like, apologize if needed. Do not act as if it never happened. People often forgive genuine errors if they see you are sincere. In contrast, trying to cover up a mistake can lead to bigger problems and could harm your image more.

---

13. Connecting with People in Person

Although much happens online, do not forget the value of meeting people face to face. Live events, local meetups, and smaller group gatherings can let you show your personality directly. If you talk to people in a friendly manner and listen to their feedback, they will remember that interaction. These personal moments can strengthen your image far more than a hundred online posts can. After all, seeing someone in real life is often more convincing than seeing them on a screen.

Try to be consistent at these events too. If your online presence is calm and kind, but you act nervous or impatient in person, people will feel a mismatch. If you need help staying calm, practice speaking in small groups first. Over time, you will gain the confidence to meet bigger crowds without losing your core traits.

14. Keeping Your Image Fresh

While you do not want to change your image all the time, you also do not want it to feel stale. Think of small updates you can make now and then to show that you are growing. For example, you might change your hairstyle slightly, refresh your outfits, or introduce a new theme to your social media content. These small adjustments can show that you are evolving in your field. Just keep them in line with your main qualities, so you do not seem like a different person overnight.

---

15. Learning from Role Models

Look at how well-known figures in your field have shaped their image. Pay attention to the choices they made. Did they pick a certain color scheme for their clothes? Do they always speak in a certain tone? How do they interact with fans online? You can learn a lot by watching others, even if you do not copy them directly. For example, if you see that a popular athlete always posts encouraging words and workout tips, and it resonates with fans, you could do something similar in your own style. Use ideas from others as a guide, but always make them your own.

---

16. Matching Your Image to Your Talent

Your personal image should match the skill or field that you want to be known for. If you are an actor, your image might show versatility and creativity. If you are a mathematician sharing your ideas, your image might be thoughtful and smart. Think about the people who will be interested in your work. What qualities do they value? If you aim to speak to families and kids, a softer, friendlier image might work better than a harsh one. If your target group is made up of serious professionals, a more formal look could make sense. Matching these things helps people feel an immediate connection with you.

---

17. Staying Professional

Professionalism means doing your work on time, being respectful, and treating your craft seriously. Even if you are presenting a fun image, you can still be professional behind the scenes. For instance, show up on time for shows or recordings, keep your commitments, and answer important messages. This might seem obvious, but many people harm their image by missing meetings or acting rudely. News about unprofessional behavior can spread quickly and damage how people see you.

Being professional also means staying organized. Keep track of your schedule, your progress, and your plans to improve. This organization can make you stand out in a good way. People will see you as reliable and easy to work with, which can bring more chances your way.

---

18. **Handling Fan Interactions**

If you start to gain fans, some might reach out with questions or comments. How you interact with them can shape your image. If your personal image includes kindness, then answering fan messages in a friendly and polite way supports that. You do not need to respond to every single message, especially if you have thousands. However, taking time to talk with your fans when possible can show that you care.

Also, remember that fans can come from many backgrounds. Some may be younger, some older. Some may share deep personal stories with you. Be polite and stay within your comfort level. If you ever feel like someone is asking too much of you or crossing your boundaries, it is okay to step back and protect your well-being. A respectful and balanced approach keeps your public image healthy.

---

19. **Dealing with Negative Media**

Once you have some recognition, you might run into negative stories or rumors. This could happen for many reasons—maybe someone misunderstood something you said, or maybe they want to harm your reputation. If you face negative media, think carefully before responding. If the claims are false, you might release a simple statement that clears things up. If the claims are partly true, address what happened, apologize if needed, and explain what you plan to do better next time.

Try not to let your emotions control you if you see negative posts. Responding in anger can make things worse. Instead, keep calm and focus on staying real. Most of the time, if you have built a genuine image, people will see through false rumors. If you made a mistake, admitting it with sincerity can actually strengthen trust in the long run.

---

20. **Growing with Your Image**

As your fame grows, your image might gain more layers. You might add new interests or talents to your public profile. Maybe you start by being known for music but later develop an interest in hosting a show. You can blend the two in a way that feels natural. The key is to let your personal image grow along with you, staying honest at each step. That way, your supporters will follow you as you explore new areas of work, because they trust the core of who you are.

A personal image is not just about clothes or a catchy phrase—it is about the whole picture of who you are, what you do, and how you treat others. When you shape that picture in a real and thoughtful way, people can see the heart behind your talent. This makes them want to stick around and support you.

Building a personal image is one of the big steps toward fame, because it is what people remember about you once they hear your name or see your face. If you do it in a way that matches your real personality, your strengths, and your values, it becomes a powerful tool to gain loyal fans and leave a strong impression. It also helps you stay consistent, which can lead to more success over time. In the next chapters, we will discuss how you can connect with others, build your skills further, and handle public attention. All these pieces work together. When you build a solid personal image alongside your plan and your talent, you set yourself up for greater recognition in the world.

CHAPTER 5: CONNECTING WITH PEOPLE

Connecting with others is a key part of becoming well-known. Even if you have strong talents, you need people who can support, guide, and introduce you to fresh chances. Making good relationships can help you learn new things and share your work with more folks. In this chapter, we will look at ways to form and keep good connections, from meeting people in your field to building meaningful ties with those who follow your work.

---

1. **Why Connections Matter**

Fame does not happen in a vacuum. Even the most skilled individuals need others to open certain doors or to spread their name. For example, if you are a singer, you might meet a person who runs a local music club. If they like you, they could invite you to perform, which can lead to more recognition. Or, if you are a writer, finding an editor you get along with can help you shape your stories so that readers enjoy them more.

At the same time, connections help you stay informed. You hear about upcoming events, open auditions, or gatherings that might be important to your field. Instead of relying only on public announcements, you get inside information. Also, when you know others, they often give you honest advice, share ideas for improvement, and direct you to places or people who can help you. This helps you grow faster than you would on your own.

---

2. **Finding the Right Places to Meet People**

To form these connections, you have to go where people in your field gather. This can be physical places or online platforms. For example, if you are an artist, you might join local art workshops or small shows in your area. If you are a musician, music lounges or open mic nights could be good spots. In the online world, there are many groups or pages where people share their work and feedback.

You do not have to limit yourself to big or famous events. Sometimes, smaller or lesser-known meetups give you a chance to have closer conversations. People are more relaxed, and it is simpler to talk about your ideas. Also, if you are just getting started, small events are less scary than huge ones. Once you gain confidence, you can explore larger gatherings where famous figures might appear.

3. **Starting Conversations**

Approaching someone you do not know can feel uncomfortable, but it is often the first step in making helpful connections. A simple greeting is enough to begin. You can mention something you both have in common, like the event you are attending. You might say, "Hi, I saw you perform earlier. I really enjoyed that song," or "I noticed your artwork on display. It had interesting colors." This breaks the ice and shows you pay attention to their work.

Try to be sincere in your compliments. People usually notice if you are just trying to flatter them. If you truly respect their skill, let them know why it caught your eye. For instance, if you are talking to another dancer, you might say, "I liked how smoothly you moved during the fast parts. It looked natural and clear." Small details show that you are genuinely interested and not just saying nice words to get something.

4. **Listening More Than You Speak**

When you start a conversation, remember that listening is as important as talking. Ask the person about their background, their interests, or what projects they have worked on. Pay attention to their answers. If you notice something that connects with your own interests, you can bring that up later. This makes the discussion feel natural, rather than forced.

People enjoy speaking about their own experiences, so letting them share can help build a sense of trust. It also helps you learn from their stories. You might get tips or warnings about mistakes to avoid. Plus, if you really listen, you can follow up with more meaningful questions, which shows you care about what they have to say.

5. **Offering Help**

A good way to form a strong bond is to see if you can help the other person in some way. It does not have to be a big offer. Maybe you have a skill they need, or you know someone who can assist them. For example, if you are good at editing videos, you could say, "If you ever need a quick edit for your clips, let me know. I would be happy to do it." This simple act can plant a seed of goodwill.

However, do not promise things you cannot do. If you say you can design a poster for their next show but have never done graphic design, you could end up harming your reputation. Be honest about what you can provide. The aim is to create a win-win situation, not to make empty promises.

---

6. **Following Up After First Contact**

Building connections is not just about that first talk. It is about staying in touch. After meeting someone, send them a short message or email saying you enjoyed talking to them. You can remind them who you are, especially if they met many people at the same event. You can also bring up anything interesting from your conversation. This might be, "I loved your idea about mixing spoken word and music. I would enjoy hearing more about it."

Try to do this follow-up soon—ideally within a few days—so they still remember you well. Keep it simple and friendly. If the person responds, you can ask if they want to meet for coffee or chat online to exchange more thoughts. Do not pressure them, though. If they seem too busy or give short responses, ease off. You do not want to appear pushy.

---

7. **Staying Genuine**

Some people approach networking only to gain things. They want to meet others solely to use them for personal benefit. This approach might get you short-term results, but it often backfires. Others can sense when you only care about what they can do for you. Over time, you might develop a bad reputation, which can block chances for real friendships or partnerships.

Instead, try to form genuine bonds. Show interest in the other person's well-being and success. If you can give them a lead or share helpful information, do it without expecting something back right away. People appreciate sincerity, and they are more likely to remember you in a positive way. In the long run, real bonds usually bring better opportunities than shallow ones.

8. **Using Online Platforms Wisely**

In modern times, many connections start online or grow there. Social media can be a powerful tool for meeting people who share your interests, even if they live far away. However, you should use it smartly. Here are some tips:

- **Create a clear profile**: Make sure your profile shows who you are and what you do. Use a friendly photo. Add a short description of your main skill or field.
- **Join groups or pages**: Look for online communities tied to your talent. For example, if you are a photographer, join photography groups. If you are an actor, find acting forums.
- **Comment and ask questions**: Be active but polite. If someone posts a video, give constructive feedback. If you see a discussion about a topic you know well, share your thoughts.
- **Stay respectful**: Online communication can be misunderstood. Use a calm tone and avoid arguments. If a discussion gets heated, think carefully before you respond.

By being active online, you can connect with people who might not be at local events. But remember to keep your personal image consistent. If you aim to be known as a warm, helpful person, make sure your online posts reflect that.

9. **Attending Workshops and Classes**

Another effective way to meet people is by joining workshops and classes in your field. Not only do you learn valuable skills, but you also meet peers and mentors. For example, if you are interested in screenwriting, you could join a local writing class. If you do well, the teacher may suggest you join a project, or classmates may invite you to collaborate.

When you take a class, try to be active. Ask questions if something is unclear. Engage in group activities. Show genuine interest in other people's work. Many friendships form in these shared learning settings. Plus, learning new techniques can make you better at your craft, which in turn can boost your path to recognition.

---

10. Joining Groups or Clubs

In addition to classes, you might find clubs or groups that meet regularly to practice or discuss your area of interest. These could be singing circles, writing clubs, or sports leagues. Regularly interacting with the same group helps you form deeper bonds because you see each other often. As you share your progress, people start to trust your efforts and might cheer you on.

You can also volunteer in some clubs or groups. For instance, if you are part of a local theater group, you could help set up the stage or handle ticket sales when you are not performing. Helping in these tasks shows you care about the collective effort, not just your own spotlight. This team spirit can create strong loyalty among members.

---

11. Learning How to Speak in Public Settings

When aiming to be recognized, you will likely speak to groups of people or do interviews. Learning to speak well in these settings can help you make a good impression. You can join a public speaking club or simply practice at smaller events. The more comfortable you become, the easier it will be to connect with audiences and potential collaborators.

Good public speaking includes:

- **Eye contact**: Look at your listeners so they feel you are addressing them.
- **Clarity**: Speak at a steady speed and volume.
- **Simple language**: Use words that everyone understands, so you do not lose them.
- **Confidence**: Stand up straight and try to stay calm, even if you feel nervous inside.

Doing this often can help you conquer fears and become better at sharing your ideas, which in turn makes you more approachable.

12. Respecting Cultural Differences

As you reach more people, you may connect with individuals from different backgrounds or countries. What seems normal to you might be different for them. For example, some cultures use direct eye contact as a sign of respect, while others view it as too bold. Some greet with handshakes, others with bows. If you travel or meet people who have different customs, try to learn a bit about their ways.

Showing respect for their traditions can help you form positive connections. Even if you make small mistakes, the fact that you tried to understand them can go a long way. This kind of awareness can open your path to a broader audience, especially if your talent has global potential.

13. Connecting with Established Figures

If you meet someone who is already known in your field, it can be both exciting and intimidating. You might worry about how to approach them. Generally, a polite introduction and a thoughtful comment about their work can break the ice. Avoid being too pushy—famous or experienced individuals may get bombarded by many requests.

Instead, try to ask a simple question about something they have worked on, or share a brief story of how their work inspired you. Show that you respect their time by keeping it short unless they invite you to speak more. Sometimes, they might be interested in your background if you come across as polite and sincere. Do not expect them to become your mentor on the spot, but you never know what can happen if you keep in touch politely over time.

14. Building a Supportive Circle

As you make connections, it is helpful to form a small circle of supportive friends or contacts who truly understand your field. These might be people at the same level as you, or some who are a bit ahead. The point is, you have a group where everyone shares tips, cheers for each other, and gives sincere feedback when needed.

A supportive circle can keep you motivated during tough times. If you face setbacks, they can remind you of your strengths. If they have faced a similar challenge, they can tell you how they handled it. This circle might also become your earliest fan base or group of collaborators. For example, you could work together on a joint project or appear together in an online video.

---

15. Avoiding Bad Crowds

While making connections is important, be careful about who you trust. Some people might appear supportive, but they could be more interested in taking advantage of you. For example, they might ask you for money to promote your work and then vanish. Or they might pressure you into doing things you are not comfortable with, claiming it will help your career.

Before you agree to anything big, do your research. Check if the person has a real track record. Read reviews or ask others who have worked with them. If a proposal sounds too good to be true, it could be a scam. It is fine to take risks in your career, but do so wisely. Learn to recognize red flags, such as vague promises or requests for large amounts of money without proof of benefits.

---

16. Using Polite Manners

Kindness and good manners never go out of style. Simple words like "please," "thank you," or "I appreciate your advice" can leave a strong mark on people. When someone helps you, acknowledge it. It might seem like a small gesture, but it builds goodwill. People enjoy being around someone who is polite and easy to work with. This can lead to more invitations and support.

Being polite also means respecting boundaries. If someone says they cannot help you right now, do not keep pushing. A polite "Thank you for your time" can keep the door open for a future chance. If you react rudely, you risk closing that door permanently.

17. **Connecting Through Social Activities**

Not all networking has to be formal or serious. Sometimes, casual social activities can create strong bonds. This could be a friendly meal after a workshop, a game night with people from your club, or a simple walk together. Relaxed settings let you see each other's personalities without stress. You might find new friends this way, and they can later point you to helpful leads.

If you get invited to a social event by someone you admire, think about going. Do not make the event all about yourself. Show interest in others, have fun conversations, and let things flow. By getting to know each other as people, you form bonds that can last longer than purely work-focused connections.

18. **Managing Your Network**

Over time, you might build many connections—online, in person, or both. It helps to keep track of who is who. You could use a simple spreadsheet or just a notebook. Write down their names, how you met, and any details you want to remember. This might seem like extra work, but it helps you recall important points when you talk again. For example, if you know someone mentioned a big project, you can ask them later, "How did that project turn out?"

Staying organized also means reaching out now and then, even if you do not need anything at that moment. A short message saying, "Hey, how have you been?" can maintain the link. People notice when you only contact them to ask for favors. So, show genuine care by staying in touch occasionally without an urgent request.

19. **Avoiding Oversharing**

When trying to connect, it is good to share about yourself so people get to know you. However, be mindful of what you reveal, especially if you are building a professional image. Talking about normal experiences or funny stories is fine, but some personal details might be best kept private. You never know how others might use that information.

If the conversation is in a public place or on a public forum, remember that many eyes might see it. Once you share something, it can be hard to take it back. Keep that in mind before you post or say anything that could harm your reputation or make you feel uneasy later.

---

20. **Growing Your Influence Through Collaboration**

One powerful way to connect with a wider audience is by collaborating with people who already have some presence. For example, if you are a painter, you could team up with a photographer to create an exhibit that blends both art forms. If you are a musician, you might work with another singer or a band to produce a joint performance. When you collaborate, you introduce each other to different sets of fans or friends.

To start a collaboration, you can contact the person, explain what you like about their work, and share a clear idea for what you want to create together. Be ready to discuss how the credit and tasks will be divided. Both sides should feel they are benefiting. If it works out well, you might both see a rise in your visibility and also form a long-term partnership.

---

21. **Handling Conflicts**

From time to time, you might have disagreements with people in your network. Perhaps you do not like a piece of advice they gave, or you think they made a decision that hurts your project. How you handle these conflicts can define your relationships moving forward. Aim to stay calm and talk things through. Share your side without accusing them. Ask for their viewpoint. Often, conflicts can be solved if both sides communicate honestly.

If the disagreement cannot be fixed, it is better to part ways politely than to engage in public fights or blame each other. Public arguments might damage your image and make others hesitant to work with you. It is acceptable to move on from someone who is not a good match for your goals and values, but do so with respect whenever possible.

---

22. Encouraging Others

When you see your friends or contacts achieve something, a simple note of support can strengthen your bond. You can send them a short message that says, "I saw you got a spot on that show—well done!" or "Your new artwork looks really nice." People appreciate being noticed, and they will remember that you took the time to encourage them. This builds mutual respect. Also, if you publicly show support (like sharing their work on your social platform), you may gain goodwill from their fans, too.

---

23. Learning Group Etiquette

In some fields, there are formal or informal rules about how to behave in a group setting. For example, in a writing group, everyone might take turns giving feedback, and you should not dominate the conversation. In a band, you need to respect each member's role and avoid overshadowing them. Understanding these unwritten rules can help you fit in better and avoid tension.

If you are new, take time to observe how others act before diving in. Ask polite questions if you are unsure about the group's usual approach. By showing you want to respect the group's ways, you are more likely to be welcomed as a valued member.

---

24. Being Memorable

Finally, once you make these connections, how do you stay in people's minds? One way is to consistently show your best qualities. If you are known for being reliable, keep your promises. If you are known for creativity, share fresh ideas often. Over time, people will recall you as someone who stands for those things.

Another approach is to keep your personal image consistent with what you have chosen for yourself, as discussed in earlier chapters.

Also, do not be afraid to share updates about your progress. If you finish a new project, let your network know. If you are performing somewhere, invite them to watch. Do this in a respectful way, without spamming. Little by little, people will see your steady development and remember that you are active and growing.

Wrapping Up Chapter 5

Connections are not only about boosting your name. They also make the path less lonely. You have folks to learn from and others to cheer for. Healthy relationships can lead you to places you might never reach alone. To form these bonds, go where your peers gather, start genuine talks, listen well, follow up politely, and offer help when you can. Use online platforms wisely, but remember to be thoughtful about how you behave there. Build a supportive circle, and be careful about who you trust. Keep politeness at the center of your interactions, and share updates about your progress so people stay aware of what you are doing.

By keeping these points in mind, you can form a reliable network that pushes you forward. In the next chapter, we will look at how to build skills and confidence, because you need both to stand out and keep moving toward wider recognition.

CHAPTER 6: BUILDING SKILLS AND CONFIDENCE

Confidence goes hand in hand with skill. Even if you know you have some talent, you might feel nervous when it is time to show it. People who watch you can sense how sure you are of yourself. A confident performer, athlete, or speaker often inspires trust and keeps people interested. At the same time, confidence without real ability can look shallow. That is why working on both skill and self-assurance is important. In this chapter, we will explore ways to improve what you do and ways to build the inner belief that you can succeed.

---

1. **Why Skill Matters**

If you want to be known for something, you need to do it well. People are drawn to those who excel, whether it is in music, dance, cooking, writing, or any other field. A high level of skill sets you apart from people who only dabble. It also helps you handle challenges that come your way. For instance, a singer with strong vocal technique can adapt to a sudden change in sound settings. A writer with polished writing habits can meet tight deadlines without losing quality.

Skill also gives you something substantial to show. If you appear on a stage or share your content online, you want people to say, "Wow, this person really knows what they are doing." That reaction can lead to support, shares, and praise, which all feed into growing your presence.

---

2. **Finding the Right Training**

Once you decide which main talent you want to develop, look for the best way to train. This might include taking lessons, joining a school that focuses on your field, or learning online through well-structured courses. If you pick a teacher or coach, choose someone who has proven skills and a teaching style that clicks with you.

Training can also happen through self-study, especially if resources for your field are limited in your area. You might watch tutorials, read step-by-step guides, or explore educational websites. The key is to follow reliable sources so you do not pick up bad habits. If you can, find a way to get feedback on your progress. Even if you learn online, you can share your work with others who have more experience. They can point out where you need to improve.

3. **Practicing Regularly**

No training plan works without constant practice. Skills take time to form, especially if you want to reach a level that stands out. Decide how much time each day or week you will devote to practice. Then, do your best to stick to that plan. Some days, you might not feel like practicing, but push through if you can. The results will show over time.

When you practice, aim for quality. Spend part of your session on areas you find tough, not just the easy parts. If you are a singer, do challenging vocal exercises to stretch your range. If you are a painter, try a technique you have never used before. Doing this helps you grow instead of staying in your comfort zone. It can feel frustrating at first, but it pays off when you see yourself getting better.

4. **Setting Progress Goals**

We talked before about having a clear plan with goals. For skill building, you can set smaller targets. For instance, if you are learning guitar, you might aim to master a certain chord progression by the end of the week. If you want to improve your free throws in basketball, you might aim for a specific percentage of accurate shots each day.

These goals keep you focused. You will have a direction each time you practice. When you meet a goal, give yourself a little sign of appreciation (like a happy remark to yourself) and then set the next one. If you miss a goal, see why it happened. Maybe you need more time, or perhaps you need a different training method. By analyzing your performance, you can adjust and keep improving.

5. **Learning from Experts**

If you can watch or listen to experts, you can pick up new strategies. This might mean studying recordings of famous performers, reading books by experienced writers, or attending workshops run by industry leaders. Notice their techniques, timing, and presentation. You do not want to copy them exactly, but you can learn a lot by observing what makes them effective.

When you see an expert at work, think about how you can try those methods in your own training. For example, if you see a pianist using a certain way of moving their hands, practice it carefully and see if it helps you play more smoothly. If you notice a top speaker organizes their points in a clear sequence, try to use a similar approach the next time you speak. This kind of thoughtful study can be a shortcut to improving fast.

6. **Staying Open to Feedback**

Feedback is vital. It tells you what is working and what is not. Sometimes, we can be too proud and only want praise. However, if you avoid criticism, you lose out on chances to get better. When a teacher or a friend points out an error, do not feel offended. View it as a chance to see something you missed. If their advice seems fair, apply it. If you disagree, it is okay to politely ask why they think so, but always remain open-minded.

Consider keeping a notebook or digital file where you collect feedback. Write down what others say you need to adjust. Then, after some time, check if you have improved in those areas. This helps you see a clear record of your progress. If the same feedback keeps coming up, it is a sign you need to focus on that specific weakness more.

7. **Building Confidence Slowly**

Confidence does not mean bragging. It means having a steady belief in your ability to handle tasks. If you have low confidence, you might hesitate to show your work or speak in front of people. If you have too much confidence, you might overlook your weaknesses. The aim is to find a balanced, realistic sense of certainty in yourself.

One way to build confidence is to start with small public displays of your skill. For example, if you want to be a public speaker, start by speaking in front of a few friends or a small club. If you want to share your singing, post a short clip online or perform at a tiny local event. Each successful attempt, no matter how modest, can boost your belief in your abilities. As you grow more at ease, you can move on to bigger stages.

8. **Dealing with Fear of Failure**

Many people do not reach their full potential because they are too worried about looking foolish or messing up. The truth is, mistakes happen to everyone. Even the best in the world fail sometimes. Instead of letting that fear stop you, think of failures as lessons. If you sing off-key during a show, figure out why. Did you not warm up properly? Did you pick a difficult song? Once you find the cause, work on it so you do better next time.

Trying something new always carries a risk of failure. But if you never try, you also never move forward. Let your mistakes guide you without crushing your spirit. Over time, your skill will improve, and those errors will happen less often. But even when they do occur, you will be better prepared to handle them calmly.

9. **Visualizing Success**

A helpful tip used by many high achievers is mental practice. Before a big performance or test, close your eyes and imagine yourself doing everything well. Picture yourself singing in tune, playing the piano notes perfectly, or delivering a smooth speech without forgetting a line. Imagine the crowd or the listeners reacting positively.

This kind of mental rehearsal can reduce nerves and improve performance. Your brain cannot always tell the difference between a real action and a detailed mental image, so it helps you feel more comfortable when the actual moment arrives. Pair this with real practice for the best results.

10. **Staying Motivated on Tough Days**

Not every day will be smooth. Sometimes you will feel tired or discouraged. Maybe progress is slower than you hoped, or you have received some harsh criticism. On such days, remind yourself of your reasons for pursuing this path. Think about the fun parts of your craft, the enjoyment it brings you, or the positive responses you have received in the past. Remembering why you started can help push you through the rough patches.

You can also try different tactics to renew your spark. For example, if you are a songwriter, try writing a tune in a new style. If you are a painter, experiment with a new color scheme. Shaking things up can bring fresh excitement. Just be careful not to lose focus on your main skill-building routine. Try something different as a small side project, and then return to your usual practice with new energy.

---

11. **Fighting Negative Self-Talk**

Sometimes, the biggest obstacle is our own thoughts. You might catch yourself thinking, "I will never be good enough" or "Everyone else is better." These words can weaken your confidence. Whenever you notice such a thought, pause and replace it with a more balanced view: "I am still learning, and I have made progress," or "I might not be at the top now, but I can get closer if I keep going."

This does not mean fooling yourself into believing you are perfect. It means giving yourself fair credit for your growth while staying aware that there is more to learn. By turning negative self-talk into more balanced statements, you train your mind to see the steps forward, not just the setbacks.

---

12. **Overcoming Stage Fright**

Stage fright is a common fear. Even people who have performed hundreds of times can feel nervous. While some level of excitement can help you deliver a better performance, too much anxiety can freeze you. One strategy is to do a mini warm-up performance for friends or family just before the actual event.

Another is to take slow, deep breaths behind the curtain or backstage to calm your racing heart.

You can also focus on a friendly face in the crowd—someone you know, or just a stranger who looks supportive. Imagine you are performing for that person alone. As you get used to the atmosphere, you may feel more at ease and start to include the rest of the audience. Over time, repeated exposure to the stage can lessen stage fright, though it might never disappear completely. Most performers learn to channel that energy into excitement rather than fear.

---

13. Taking Care of Your Body and Mind

Building skill requires more than just training the specific talent. It also means keeping your body and mind in good shape. If you are always exhausted or stressed, it will show in your work. Make sure you get enough rest, eat meals that nourish you, and do some exercise if that helps your overall wellness. A clear mind and a healthy body often lead to better learning and better performances.

If you feel worn out, it can be useful to set aside a day or two for rest. During that time, do activities that help you relax. Some people enjoy simple walks or reading. Others might like mild exercise or calm music. The aim is to return to practice with fresh energy. Overworking yourself can lead to burnout, which hurts both skill development and confidence.

---

14. Joining Friendly Competitions

Competitions can be a way to test your progress. If you are a singer, you might enter a local singing contest. If you are a cook, you might compete in a neighborhood cooking challenge. These events push you to perform under pressure, which is good practice for bigger stages. They also let you see what others in your field are doing, giving you fresh ideas.

However, remember that losing a competition does not mean you lack ability. Judges might be looking for specific traits. Your style could be different from what they want. Winning is nice, but the real value is in the experience of competing, learning from others, and performing in front of a wider audience.

15. **Using Self-Recording Tools**

One great way to see your strengths and weaknesses is by recording yourself. This can be done easily with a phone or computer. If you are a speaker, record a short talk. If you are a dancer, record your practice. Then watch the video to note what went well and what needs fixing. You might notice that you move awkwardly at a certain point or that your voice is too soft at times.

Video review allows you to become your own critic. You can look at a performance more objectively. Sometimes we think we did poorly, but when we watch the replay, it looks better than we felt. Other times, we think we nailed something but see errors on camera. Either way, these insights help you improve more effectively than just guessing.

16. **Seeking Mentors for Deeper Guidance**

Sometimes, a teacher in a group setting is not enough. If you can, try to find a mentor who works with you one-on-one. This might be a well-known performer, a retired athlete, a top coach, or a seasoned writer. Mentors can share wisdom from their own ups and downs, helping you avoid pitfalls and speed up your growth.

When you meet a potential mentor, show respect for their experience. Be clear about what you hope to learn. Also, be ready to put in the effort they expect. If you do not follow their advice or skip practice, they might lose interest in helping you. Mentorship is a partnership: they give you knowledge, and you show your appreciation by working hard and improving.

17. **Handling Plateaus**

A plateau is when you feel your progress has stopped. You are practicing, but you do not see improvement. This can be frustrating. One approach is to try a fresh method of training. If you usually learn by reading, try learning with videos or hands-on exercises. If you keep practicing the same pieces of music, learn a new piece that challenges you in a different way.

You can also ask someone new to evaluate your work. A fresh pair of eyes or ears might spot an area where you can improve. Sometimes, changing your routine or environment can break the plateau. If you always practice in your room, go to a park or a friend's place. The shift can spark new motivation.

18. Comparing Yourself Fairly

It is natural to look at others in your field and feel envy if they are ahead. But comparisons can kill your confidence if you do it too often. Remember that everyone has a different background, different hours put in, and different personal circumstances. A better approach is to compare your present self to your past self. Ask: "Am I better than I was last month?" If the answer is yes, that is real progress.

When you see someone who is far ahead, treat it as inspiration rather than a reason to feel bad. You can learn from them, adapt their methods, and remember that they likely spent years reaching that level. Use their success to set a vision for yourself, but do not let it make you feel like you will never get there.

19. Displaying Your Skills More Often

Part of building confidence is getting used to showing your skill. This could be through small events, online postings, or casual demos for friends. The more often you let others see your work, the more natural it will feel. You might get nervous at first, but each time you do it, you gain a bit more ease. Over time, performing or sharing in public can become second nature.

Posting your work online also allows you to gather feedback from a bigger audience. You can see which pieces or styles people like the most. However, be careful with negative or rude comments. Some people online are not trying to help. Decide whose feedback is worth taking seriously and ignore the rest. Focus on comments from those who have some knowledge of your field or give constructive thoughts.

20. **Sticking to Good Habits**

Once you have built some skills, keep them by staying consistent with your practice and learning. It is easy to become lazy when you feel comfortable. You might think, "I am good enough now," and practice less. This can make your progress stall or even decline. Try to keep challenging yourself, even if you are getting positive attention. The ones who remain at the top keep practicing.

Having a routine can help you stay on track. For example, decide that every weekday morning you do an hour of practice, or every evening before bed you work on a new piece of writing. Keep that pattern unless you have a good reason to skip. Also, continue to seek fresh tasks that expand your range of abilities. When you keep learning, you also keep your mind active and your confidence growing.

---

21. **Finding Joy in the Process**

Improving your skill should not be pure drudgery. Yes, it can be tiring at times, but try to find enjoyment in the steps you take. If singing is your focus, find songs that excite you. If you are a comedian, test new jokes on supportive friends to hear their laughter. That sense of fun can keep you motivated during tough periods. Also, when you enjoy what you do, your performances often come across as more genuine.

Do not forget to give yourself small breaks or do something fun outside of your main talent. A balanced life can keep you from feeling fed up with constant practice. When you return to your main skill, you might have a fresh perspective. This balance can make you a more well-rounded person, which often makes your performances or creations even stronger.

---

22. **Staying Humble**

Confidence does not mean looking down on others. Being good at something does not entitle you to treat anyone poorly. If you become known for arrogance, it can ruin your relationships and make people dislike working with you. Try to keep a sense of humility. Recognize that many people have helped you get where you are, from teachers to friends to audience members who gave you a chance.

Humility also means staying open to learning. Even if you are skilled, there could be a new style or method you have not tried. Be willing to learn from people who are younger or less famous, too. Sometimes, fresh talent has bright ideas. The more open you stay, the more you can keep growing in your field.

---

23. **Reviewing Your Growth**

Every month or so, take time to look back at your improvements. Watch old videos or read old work if you have it. Notice how your voice, style, or approach has changed. Seeing concrete proof of growth can fuel your confidence and show you that your practice is working. It can also highlight areas where you are still stuck.

By doing this regularly, you keep track of your path. You can celebrate small wins within yourself, which helps you stay positive. You can also plan new goals based on what you have noticed. It becomes a cycle of progress, review, adjust, and move forward again.

---

24. **Combining Skill with Confidence for Recognition**

When you have a strong skill set and a steady confidence, it shows. People see your skills through your results—whether that is a performance, a game, a product, or an artwork. They see your confidence in how you handle yourself—calm, focused, and open to interaction. This blend can attract fans, supporters, and even sponsors who see value in what you bring to the table.

As you become more visible, you might get asked to speak at events, teach workshops, or be interviewed. Use these chances wisely. Show that you know your craft well, and present it in a way that is easy for others to follow. If they leave with a good impression, they will remember your name and possibly share it with more people.

Wrapping Up Chapter 6

Building skill and confidence is not an instant process. It requires time, ongoing effort, and the willingness to push through failure. You need to practice regularly, stay open to feedback, and keep a balanced mind so you do not get discouraged. Confidence grows when you see real improvement in your abilities, and skill grows when you practice with purpose and learn from experts or mentors.

Both of these factors feed each other: as your skill rises, you feel more confident; as your confidence increases, you perform or create better, which further sharpens your abilities. This cycle can carry you forward, helping you reach levels of excellence that bring you closer to the recognition you want. In upcoming chapters, we will focus on other aspects that support your aim, such as handling public attention, dealing with doubt, and using various platforms to expand your reach. By merging strong talent with a healthy dose of self-belief, you will be better equipped to make the most of every chance that comes your way.

CHAPTER 7: STUDYING GOOD EXAMPLES

Learning from people who have already done well in your field can save you time and help you grow faster. While you do not want to copy them exactly, you can watch what they do right and see how parts of their approach might fit you. This chapter will talk about how to find, observe, and learn from good examples. It will also cover how to make sure you keep your own voice, so you do not lose your uniqueness.

---

1. **Why Look at Good Examples?**
   When you try to figure things out alone, you might spend a lot of time guessing what works. However, if you look at those who have reached a high level in the area you want to be known for—such as music, acting, writing, sports, or online content—you can see methods that already work. You can also see mistakes they made before they became well-known. This can warn you about what not to do.

Good examples also inspire you. When you notice someone who came from a similar place or faced struggles like yours, it can give you hope. It shows that hard work and smart choices can pay off. Observing people who do things well can spark ideas you might not think of on your own. You might notice their style, schedule, or ways of speaking to fans. These details can guide your own approach in ways that feel natural for you.

---

2. **Finding the Right People to Study**
   Not all role models are the same. You want to look for people who are respected for reasons that match your goals. For instance, if you want to be a thoughtful writer, you might not gain much by studying a writer known mostly for controversy. If you want to be a calm public speaker, you may not want to focus on someone who shouts or shocks the crowd to get attention. Instead, choose individuals who have success in the style or approach you admire.

Start by making a list of well-known folks in your field. You can do this by reading blogs, asking friends, or searching on video platforms. From that list, see which ones line up with how you want to grow. Maybe you are drawn to one person's creative style, another's strong sense of humor, and a third's professional attitude. You can learn different lessons from each one.

3. **Reading Biographies and Watching Interviews**
   Many well-known people share their thoughts through interviews, articles, or even books about their lives. These stories can be very helpful. They often talk about their early days, their struggles, and the choices that led them toward a bigger stage. By reading their words or watching them on camera, you learn about their values and how they solved problems.

Pay special attention to the steps they took when things were uncertain. Did they move to a different city? Did they practice a certain number of hours each day? Did they get a mentor who guided them? Also note any big challenges they mention—such as money problems, rejections, or personal setbacks. Seeing how they handled those moments can prepare you if you face something similar.

4. **Studying Their Public Performances or Work**
   Apart from reading about their lives, you can also look at their actual work. For instance, if you admire a famous singer, listen to their live concerts or recorded songs. Notice how they control their voice, how they interact with the band, and how they communicate with the audience. If you look up to a dancer, study their footwork, their timing, and the emotion they show on stage.

It can be helpful to watch or read more than once. On your first look, you might just enjoy the performance. On the second look, focus on specific details. For example, if you are studying an actor, pick a scene and see how they use their eyes or facial expressions. If you are studying an online creator, notice how they edit their videos or talk to the camera. By breaking down the performance, you start to see patterns that made them shine.

5. **Taking Notes and Organizing Your Thoughts**
   As you study these examples, it is smart to keep notes. You can use a notebook or a file on your computer. Write down what stands out. You might list a technique you see—such as a trick for controlling the stage, a special practice method, or a clever way of speaking. Make sure to also note what you think of it: Do you like it? Could you do something similar?

This record helps you remember details you might forget later. It also keeps you from mixing up the approaches of different role models. Maybe you have one page for each person you are watching. Then, from time to time, you can look over your notes and see which ideas you could adapt for your own work. Over time, these small details can add up to big improvements in how you present yourself or shape your material.

---

6. **Comparing Different Styles**
   Not every successful person follows the same path. One comedian might use a clean, friendly style, while another might use silliness or more direct humor. Both might be well-liked, even though their styles are different. By comparing a few people, you see that success can come in many forms. This reminds you that you do not have to mold yourself into the exact shape of one person. You can take bits and pieces that suit you best.

Comparing styles also helps you avoid copying someone too much. If you only look at one example, you might end up sounding like a weak version of that person. But if you look at several, you can pick up a range of ideas and mix them in a way that still feels natural for you. This is how you build your own unique style, guided by examples but not controlled by them.

---

7. **Looking for Patterns in Their Behavior**
   When you watch enough interviews or read enough stories, you might notice certain patterns in how successful people behave. For example, many of them talk about staying focused, practicing often, and being open to feedback. Some mention that they do not give up when they fail the first time. Others talk about having a solid team or group of friends around them who give honest advice and support.

These patterns are not magic tricks. They are habits or mindsets that often lead to good results, like discipline, patience, or kindness. Even though each person's success story is unique, these patterns show up again and again. That is a clue that they might be important. Think about which patterns you can use in your own life.

8. **Learning from Their Mistakes**
   Success stories often include mistakes, big and small. Some famous athletes may have had a period where they lost a lot of matches or got injured and had to adapt. Some actors may have gone through a phase where no one would hire them. By reading or watching them talk about these tough times, you see that even the best face low points. More importantly, you see what they did to come back stronger.

Try not to feel glad about their failures, but do note how they reacted. Did they work even harder? Did they learn a new skill to overcome a problem? Did they switch gears and aim for a slightly different path? By observing these lessons, you might avoid the same pitfalls or, at least, handle them with more wisdom if they happen to you.

9. **Observing Their Interactions with Fans and Media**
   If you want to be well-known, part of that involves dealing with the public. Study how your chosen role models handle interviews, press conferences, or fan questions online. Do they keep a polite and calm tone, even when questions are tough? Do they show gratitude to the people who support them? How do they respond to critics?

Some famous people are known for being rude or defensive, which can harm their image. Others are known for staying calm, witty, or respectful. If you see someone handle a difficult reporter with grace, take note of how they did it. That skill might help you someday. You can also watch how they connect with fans—maybe by signing autographs, answering questions on social media, or doing small acts of kindness. These habits can build a solid reputation.

10. **Watching How They Keep Their Energy**
    Many high achievers have busy schedules. They perform or work almost every day, travel often, and might face lots of stress. Notice how they take care of themselves. Some talk about getting enough sleep, eating well, or doing simple exercises to stay fit. Others might mention having hobbies that help them relax.

You do not need to copy everything they do, but it is good to be aware of ways people stay balanced. If you overwork and ignore your health, you might burn out. Studying someone who handles a busy life well can guide you in setting your own habits. Maybe you cannot match their exact routine, but you can pick a few tips that fit your life, like setting aside time for rest or gentle exercise.

---

11. **Seeing Their Consistency**
    Another thing you might notice in good examples is consistency. They often show up on time, deliver solid performances, or produce new material regularly. They do not suddenly vanish for long periods without explanation. This reliability builds trust with fans and with people in their industry.

Look at how they keep this consistency. Do they follow a daily schedule? Do they have assistants or managers who keep things organized? Even if you do not have a big team, you can adopt the mindset of consistency by making a personal routine. For instance, if you want to post online content to gain recognition, pick a schedule you can handle—maybe once a week—and stick to it. Observing a consistent role model can remind you that steady effort often leads to better results over time.

---

12. **Studying Their Style and Branding**
    People who stand out often have a clear style or image that people connect with. This can be seen in the clothes they wear, the colors they use in their online posts, or the tone of their public messages. They usually keep it fairly uniform so that others quickly recognize them. When you look at good examples, ask yourself how they built this style. Is it playful or formal? Do they use bright visuals or calm ones?

While you do not want to copy someone else's exact style, you can learn about the importance of clarity. For example, if a musician always wears a certain color or has a certain stage layout, fans recognize it. This memory factor can be helpful if you also want to be instantly recognizable. You might not choose the same colors or outfits, but you can think about how to create a clear, simple style of your own.

13. **Looking at Their Teamwork**
    Many successful people do not work alone. They might have band members, writing partners, coaches, or managers. Even if they appear solo in front of the camera, there is often a team helping them plan or produce. Try to see how they interact with these partners. Do they delegate tasks well? Do they treat their helpers kindly?

Seeing how someone handles teamwork can teach you a lot about leadership and group dynamics. You might learn how to communicate ideas clearly or how to show respect for each person's role. This is important because, as you grow in your field, you will likely need others to assist you or collaborate with you. If you have a good model for teamwork, it can keep your group strong and positive.

14. **Adapting Their Methods to Fit Your Life**
    After you gather insights, you have to decide which ones to try. Remember, you do not live the same life as your role model. You might have a different schedule, different resources, or different personal responsibilities. So, take their advice or habits and shape them to fit your situation.

For example, if your favorite actor says they practice lines for four hours every morning, but you have a day job, you might not be able to match that. Instead, you could practice lines for one hour in the morning and one hour at night. The idea is to keep the spirit of their technique—regular practice—rather than force yourself into their exact lifestyle.

15. **Staying True to Your Own Voice**
    A big risk in studying other people's work is losing yourself. If you try to mirror them too closely, your unique qualities might fade. Fans can usually tell if someone is just copying a bigger name. Also, you will likely be happier (and more original) if you let your own thoughts and style shine through.

To avoid copying, always ask yourself: "Does this method feel natural to me? Can I shape it in a way that feels right?" If the answer is no, it might not be a good fit. There is nothing wrong with admiring someone else's approach, but you want to adapt it so that it blends with who you already are.

---

16. **Keeping an Open Mind**
    It is fine to have favorite role models, but be careful not to ignore others who might also teach you something valuable. Sometimes, a person you do not follow closely might have a very clever trick or method that can help you. If you shut out everyone except your main favorites, you might miss out on fresh ideas.

This is why it can be good to watch a variety of examples, even outside your main field. For instance, if you are a musician, you could look at a public speaker's way of engaging the crowd, or if you are a writer, you might learn about story flow from a filmmaker. Inspiration can come from many places, not just the exact path you are on.

---

17. **Avoiding Idol Worship**
    While it is helpful to study good examples, do not put anyone on a pedestal. Even your heroes have flaws and might make choices you do not agree with. If you set them up as perfect, you could feel crushed if they do something disappointing. Also, if you think of them as too perfect, you might doubt your own ability to reach their level.

Look at your role models as humans who achieved something notable, not as impossible legends. That makes their achievements more relatable. It also helps you keep a balanced view: you can learn from their strong points and avoid copying their mistakes. Remember that you are also capable of great things if you work hard and stay focused.

18. **Watching Out for Changing Times**
    Some role models found success in a different era. For example, maybe a certain TV star rose to fame when there were fewer channels, or a writer became well-known before the internet changed the way we read. While their basic lessons might still be valid (like being disciplined or connecting with audiences), their exact path might not apply in today's world.

If you study older examples, try to figure out which parts still work now. The same goes for brand-new examples. Maybe someone got famous quickly through a platform that is popular at the moment, but that might change in the future. Keep your eyes on the core lessons—things like skill, consistency, kindness, and a strong work ethic—rather than the temporary details.

19. **Seeing the Value of Persistence**
    When you look at enough success stories, you will notice that many of these people tried again and again, even when they failed at first. Some had many rejections from agencies or producers. Some posted videos for years before anyone really noticed them. Persistence seems to be a common thread.

Learning about their slow climb can keep you going on days when you feel like you are not moving forward fast enough. You might think, "This actor was turned down ten times before they got a small role, and I have only been turned down twice." Keeping that in mind helps you stay patient. Progress can be slow, but if you keep learning and trying, you can get closer to your goals.

20. **Mixing New Ideas and Tradition**
    Many role models respect both the old ways and new ways in their field. For example, a modern musician might still study classic artists to learn strong fundamentals, then add a modern twist to stay fresh. A new writer might read older novels to understand tried-and-true storytelling

methods, then experiment with current themes to speak to today's readers.

When studying good examples, note how they balance tradition with innovation. Some lean more heavily on tradition, some push forward with modern ideas, and some do both. Think about which balance you want to strike. Maybe you like the classic approach, or maybe you like blending that approach with new technology or popular trends.

---

21. **Learning Networking Skills from Them**

    Besides their main talent, people who are well-known often have good networking skills. They might connect with others in their industry, speak politely to important figures, or show up at events that expand their reach. Look for clues about how they built these relationships. Maybe they started by contacting a small local place, or maybe they volunteered their time at events where they could meet people.

These stories can teach you how to create your own path. If someone used local shows to gain a following, maybe that is something you can do. If they mention that they wrote to many people but only got a reply from a few, that is a lesson in not giving up. Follow their examples with your own spin, and do not forget to maintain a sincere attitude.

---

22. **Checking Their Early Work**

    Sometimes, it is easy to only see someone's polished, modern performances. But if you can find their early work—maybe their first songs, first short films, or first stand-up comedy sets—you might be surprised. Often, they were not as smooth or impressive at the beginning. That can give you comfort, realizing that they grew over time, just like you are trying to do.

Try to see how they went from that early stage to their current stage. Did they change their style? Did their skill level increase after working with a certain teacher? Did they switch teams or move to a new location? Seeing the steps can be more informative than just admiring their high-level moments. It breaks it down into smaller moves that you can learn from.

23. **Keeping a Balanced View of Media Hype**
    When someone is famous, the media might praise them as though everything they do is perfect. Or, in other cases, the media might focus on their mistakes. Either way, try not to get swept away by the hype or the harsh judgment. Look for direct sources, like interviews where they speak for themselves, or official accounts of their work. If you rely on gossip or headlines alone, you might miss the real story of how they became skilled.

It is good to be aware that the media can shape or twist the view of someone. So, balance your research by reading different sources. Talk to people who know more about the field. Sometimes, an overlooked figure might have great lessons to teach, but they do not get the flashy headlines that bigger names do. Keep your mind open to lesser-known but still high-quality examples too.

24. **Putting What You Learn into Action**
    Finally, the main reason for studying good examples is to make your own progress. Take the notes, ideas, and observations you have gathered and try them in your practice or performances. Do not just watch passively—use what you have learned. Set small tasks for yourself, like applying a new technique in your next show or trying a new training routine for a week.

If you discover that something really helps you, stick with it. If it feels awkward or does not work at all, move on. Over time, you will build a personal method that blends your natural strengths with the insights you found by studying others. This is what creates your unique path, guided by the wisdom of those who have gone before you but still shaped by your own voice and choices.

Wrapping Up Chapter 7

Studying good examples is about learning from success and failures alike. It is about understanding the patterns that tend to bring results, from strong work habits to consistent presentation. It also means looking at how people handle pressure, adapt to changes, and treat others. By watching, reading, and taking notes with an open mind, you can gather valuable tips that will speed up your growth.

Keep in mind that you are not trying to become a clone of anyone. You still have your own personality and talent, which you want to show the world. Watching others simply teaches you what is possible and what to watch out for. In the next chapter, we will discuss how to handle public attention once your name starts to spread. That can be both exciting and stressful, but with the right strategies, you can stay balanced and make the most of being recognized.

CHAPTER 8: HANDLING PUBLIC ATTENTION

Once you start getting recognized, you may find yourself in front of more eyes and ears than ever. People might talk about you, share your content, or ask you for your views on certain topics. While attention can be flattering, it also comes with new pressures. You might worry about making mistakes, pleasing fans, or handling critics. This chapter looks at how to manage public attention in a way that protects your well-being and helps you stay on track.

---

1. **Understanding the Nature of Public Attention**
    When people first notice you, it might feel strange. One day, you are just doing your own thing, and the next, strangers might be complimenting you or even pointing out flaws. The first step is to know that public attention often changes quickly. One month, you might be popular because of a viral post; the next, everyone could be watching someone else. Fame can rise or fall, so try not to let it define your entire sense of self.

Public attention is also rarely 100% positive. Some folks will like you, some will criticize you, and some will not care either way. That is normal. No one is liked by everyone, and that includes the most famous stars. Accepting this fact can help you approach attention with a calmer mind. You do not need to be perfect or please everybody.

---

2. **Staying True to Your Core Values**
    When you get attention, there might be pressure to act or speak in ways that do not feel right. Maybe some people want you to be more dramatic than you normally are, or they want you to say things that might attract more clicks but do not match your real beliefs. It is important to remember why you started on this path in the first place.

Keep a clear sense of your values and your personal style. If you act fake, you will struggle to keep up the act over time. Audiences can often sense when someone is being dishonest. Also, changing yourself too much to satisfy a trend can leave you feeling empty once that trend passes. Being real might lose a few fans who want something else, but it will gain you loyal supporters who appreciate who you are.

---

3. **Dealing with Opinions**
   As you become more visible, you will hear more opinions—both good and bad. You might get glowing reviews or harsh comments. One approach is to read or listen to feedback that seems helpful, while ignoring rude or hateful remarks. Not all opinions are created equal. Some people offer genuine points on how you can improve. Others might just want to cause trouble.

If you find yourself upset by negative remarks, remember that they do not define you. Also, take a step back: Is there anything constructive in the criticism? Sometimes, a critic's tone might be harsh, but they might raise a fair point, such as needing to speak more clearly or choose better topics. If so, you can learn from it. If not, let it go. You do not have to argue with every person who disagrees with you.

---

4. **Setting Boundaries**
   More attention can mean more people trying to reach you—through messages, at events, or even in public places. While being friendly is good, you also need to protect your privacy and sanity. Set boundaries about what you will share. Decide which parts of your personal life are off-limits. If you feel uneasy when strangers ask personal questions, it is okay to politely say you prefer not to talk about that.

You might also have to limit how many messages you answer. If you get hundreds of comments or questions, you cannot respond to them all. That does not make you a bad person. You can focus on a few questions that stand out or set a certain amount of time each day to go through messages. Having rules keeps you from feeling overwhelmed.

---

5. **Handling Crowds and Live Events**
   As you grow in fame, you might be invited to speak or perform in front of

large groups. This can be exciting but also nerve-racking. To handle crowds better, prepare well. Know what you want to say or do. Arrive early if you can, so you can get a feel for the space. Some people like to do quick breathing exercises or quietly rehearse behind the stage.

When you are on stage or at a meetup, try to engage the audience. Make eye contact, smile, or respond kindly if someone shouts a question. If you get nervous, focus on a few friendly faces. That can help you feel like you are talking to friends rather than a sea of strangers. After the event, if people line up to meet you, try to be patient, but also pay attention to your energy. If you need a break, let an organizer know.

6. **Responding to Media Requests**
   If your profile rises, reporters or bloggers might want interviews. They could ask you about your work, your personal life, or even your thoughts on bigger social issues. Before you speak with them, have a clear idea of what you feel comfortable sharing. You do not have to answer every question in full detail. If you do not know something, it is fine to say so. If you are not prepared to discuss a certain area, politely redirect the conversation.

Watch out for tricky questions where the reporter might be aiming for a sensational headline. If you sense that, respond carefully or say something neutral. It also helps to keep your tone calm. If a question seems aggressive, answer in a measured way. Losing your temper can lead to negative stories about you. Remember, once you say something in an interview, it can be repeated in many places.

7. **Managing Online Platforms**
   Social media or video channels can play a big part in your fame. As people follow you, the comments section can become busy. You might see words of praise, questions, or even hateful language. It is your choice whether to moderate your pages. Some well-known people have rules for commenting, such as removing offensive posts. Others prefer to allow free discussion. Think about what feels best for you, as the owner of the platform.

It is wise to keep track of how social media affects your feelings. If checking your comments too often makes you sad or angry, give yourself limits. For example, you might only check comments once a day or turn off notifications. You should be in control of your online use, not the other way around. Some people even hire a helper to manage their accounts once they have a big audience, but this might not be possible or necessary for everyone.

---

8. **Facing Rumors or False News**

    With more attention comes the risk of rumors. Someone might spread a story that you said or did something you never did. Or they might twist your words. First, decide whether the rumor is worth addressing. If only a few people believe it and it does not hurt your reputation, sometimes ignoring it is better, so you do not give it more spotlight.

If the rumor grows and can affect you badly, consider making a clear statement. Explain the truth in simple words, maybe on your official pages. Keep it short and factual. Trying to argue every detail might make the rumor bigger. Also, avoid attacking the people who spread it. Show calmness and honesty. People who trust you will likely believe your side of the story. Those who want to hate might keep hating, no matter what you say.

---

9. **Staying Grounded Around Flattery**

    When people admire you, they might praise you a lot. Compliments feel good, but too much flattery can create an inflated sense of self. You risk becoming arrogant or forgetting that you still have areas to improve. It is important to stay balanced. You can appreciate kind words but also remember that you are still learning.

Keep close friends or family members who knew you before the attention. They can give you honest views and keep you in touch with your roots. If you surround yourself only with people who say you are the best at everything, you might lose the drive to improve. A bit of healthy humility helps you grow your skill and stay relatable to fans.

---

10. **Protecting Your Emotional Health**
    Getting recognized can bring stress. You might feel pressure to keep pleasing your audience or to keep performing at a high level. If you start feeling exhausted or anxious, pay attention to those signs. Take breaks when needed. Talk to a trusted friend, counselor, or family member if stress becomes heavy. Do not feel ashamed if you need support. Lots of famous people speak about the anxiety or sadness they face behind the scenes.

If you find that social media or certain events cause you distress, step back. Your well-being matters more than always being available. Also, keep up hobbies or interests that bring you peace but are not tied to your public image. This gives you a space to relax and stay yourself when you are not in the spotlight.

---

11. **Knowing When to Say "No"**
    As you gain attention, you might receive more offers—interviews, guest spots, brand partnerships, or even requests from charities. While it can be tempting to say yes to everything, you risk becoming overwhelmed. You also risk spreading yourself too thin, causing your main work to suffer. Learn to say "no" when something does not fit your goals, your schedule, or your values.

Saying "no" can be done politely. Thank the person for the offer, but explain that you do not have the time or that it is not the right fit at the moment. People might be disappointed, but they often respect honesty. Trying to do too much can lead to burnout or sloppy results, which is not good for anyone in the long run.

---

12. **Staying in Touch with Supporters**
    While you cannot talk to everyone, letting your fans know you appreciate them can go a long way. You might post a short thank-you note, share small updates on your progress, or hold occasional live chats if you have time. This makes supporters feel included. They are, after all, a big part of why you are recognized.

If fans send you positive messages or creative gifts (like fan art), acknowledge it when possible. You do not have to send an in-depth reply to each person, but a general post saying "I am grateful for all of you" can warm people's hearts. When they see you notice their support, they are likely to keep cheering you on. Just be careful not to promise personal contact you cannot maintain. Honesty keeps expectations healthy.

---

13. **Handling Pressure to Keep Growing**
    Once you have some fame, you might feel an urge to grow your numbers even more—whether it is followers, ticket sales, or viewers. That can be a strong pull, and it might push you to try new methods or produce more content than you can handle. While growth is nice, do not forget the reason you started your creative or skill-based path in the first place.

If all you think about is staying on top, you might lose the joy or spark that made you special. People often follow someone because they sense real passion or genuine skill. If you let stress overshadow that passion, your work might feel forced. It is okay to aim higher, but balance that with steady work and a focus on quality. Growth will often happen more naturally if you keep doing good work and maintaining your authenticity.

---

14. **Keeping Private Relationships Safe**
    Attention can affect your friends and family too. They might get questions about you or feel uneasy if fans contact them for information. Talk to them about how much they want to be in the public eye. Some might love to support you openly, while others prefer to stay in the background. Respect their comfort level.

If you are in a close relationship, be aware that your schedule or public duties might cause strain. Make time to connect with your loved ones in a relaxed environment. Let them know you value them not just as part of your image, but as real people who have always been there for you. This balance can keep your home life and public life from clashing too much.

---

15. **Avoiding Arguments Online**
    The internet is full of conflicts. When you are known, people might pull you into heated discussions or ask you to take sides on issues. While sharing opinions can be meaningful, fighting publicly often does more harm than good. It can distract from your main work and create negative energy around your name.

If you must address a serious topic, try to do so calmly. Present your view, allow for other views, and step away if things turn hostile. Remember that you do not have to respond to every comment. Sometimes, being silent on a post is better than fueling arguments that cannot be solved through online bickering.

---

16. **Being Mindful of What You Post**
    As a recognized figure, your posts can spread quickly. A joke that seems harmless to you might offend some people. A photo that reveals too much about where you live might draw unwanted attention. Think about what you share before you hit "send."

This does not mean you must live in fear of every post. Rather, just pause and ask, "Is this something I want everyone to see? Will I be okay with this post a year from now?" If you have doubts, it might be safer not to post it. This self-check can prevent problems and keep your public image more stable.

---

17. **Finding Mentors or Advisors for This Stage**
    Just like you might have mentors for your skill, you can look for mentors to help you handle fame. Some public figures specialize in guiding rising talent on dealing with attention, press, or brand deals. If you can find someone who has navigated fame successfully, they might offer tips you would never think of alone.

Be cautious, though. Make sure the mentor has a good reputation and truly wants to help you. You do not need someone who only cares about shaping you into a money-making product. Look for someone who respects your individuality and understands your field. Their advice on contracts, personal conduct, and media handling could save you from major blunders.

18. **Using Your Voice for Positive Impact**
    When you have people listening, you have a chance to do good. Some well-known individuals use their platforms to bring attention to causes they believe in—like helping animals, supporting kids' programs, or promoting healthy habits. If you feel strongly about something that aligns with your values, you can mention it to your supporters, as long as you do it with care.

Be mindful that whatever you support, you should understand it well. If you promote a cause without knowing the facts, you could face backlash. Also, not everyone will agree with you. That is okay. You can still share what you stand for in a polite way. Doing so can deepen your connection with fans who share your views, and it might encourage positive deeds.

---

19. **Learning to Handle Fame Gaps**
    Public attention is not always steady. You might have a surge of interest after releasing a big project, then a quieter period. This up-and-down cycle is normal. During a lull, you can focus on improving your craft, planning your next move, or spending more time with friends and family. Instead of feeling you are losing relevance, see it as a time to rest and plan.

During a low-attention phase, you might also experiment with new ideas without as much scrutiny. Sometimes, that is when creativity can flourish. Then, when you have something fresh to share, you can step back into the spotlight.

---

20. **Handling Comparisons with Others**
    As you get recognized, people might compare you to others in your field: "So-and-so is better than you," or "You are the next [famous person]." This can be flattering or annoying. Either way, remember that you have your own style and timeline. Comparisons can stir up jealousy or a sense of competition that takes away your focus from your true goals.

If someone tries to bait you with comparisons in an interview or online, you can respond kindly: "We have different strengths, and I respect their work. I am just doing my best." This shows you are not interested in petty feuds. It also conveys confidence that you know your own path without putting the other person down.

---

21. **Dealing with Entitled Demands**
    As your name grows, some folks might demand special favors. They might say, "You should do this for me for free" because you are known, or they might expect you to appear at their event for no compensation. Decide where you draw the line. If you do not feel comfortable doing something for free, politely decline or request a fair arrangement.

It is also okay to offer help if you truly want to, such as supporting a charity you care about. Just make sure you do it because it aligns with your values, not because someone pressured you. Staying clear about these boundaries protects your time and respect.

---

22. **Finding Balance and Hobbies**
    Though you might be recognized for one main talent, do not lose sight of other parts of your life. Having hobbies unrelated to your public image helps you unwind. It might be drawing, cooking at home, playing a casual sport with friends, or simply reading. These private interests give you a place to be yourself without the pressure of onlookers.

Balance also means managing your finances well, if you start earning more. People who rise fast can sometimes misuse their money or trust the wrong person. Find reliable advice on budgeting or saving so you do not end up in financial trouble down the road. It is easier to keep doing what you love if your personal life is stable.

---

23. **Being Ready for Possible Criticism from People You Know**
    Sometimes, people close to you might feel jealous or resentful once you gain attention. They might say hurtful things or distance themselves. This can be painful, but it is a reality for some who become known. Keep calm. If you can, talk to them honestly. Let them know you still care about

them. But if they continue to behave badly, you might have to accept that their actions are not something you can control.

Focus on keeping supportive people around you. Not everyone will cheer for your success, and that is not your fault. As long as you are treating people well, you can move forward with a clear mind. Those who truly care will stay in your life in a positive way.

---

24. **Enjoying the Good Side of Attention**
    Even though attention can be stressful, it also has perks. You can share your ideas with a bigger audience, meet interesting people, and open new doors for your projects. The key is to keep it in perspective and remember that your sense of worth should not rely completely on how many people are watching.

Enjoy the kindness people show you. Enjoy the fact that your talent is being noticed. Use the attention to improve your craft and, if it fits your vision, to support causes or messages you believe in. If you keep a healthy mindset, public attention can be a tool to help you reach your larger aims, rather than a trap that controls your life.

Wrapping Up Chapter 8
Handling public attention involves setting boundaries, staying authentic, and looking after your emotional health. You will run into critics, maybe even rumors, but you can address those challenges with calm and tact. You do not have to share every detail of your private life or please everyone who has an opinion. By keeping your values clear, you can enjoy the benefits of being recognized while limiting the downsides.

In the next chapters, we will continue looking at topics that shape a balanced path toward fame. We will explore how to deal with doubt, use different media formats, reach the right audience, and more. As you move through this process, remember that your own well-being and the quality of your work are more important than chasing approval from every new face. If you stay rooted in who you are, you can make public attention a positive part of your effort to become and remain well-known.

CHAPTER 9: DEALING WITH DOUBT

Doubt can come at any time—whether you are just starting your path to fame or already have a foothold. It can arise from within yourself, from people around you, or from seeing others who seem far ahead. This doubt might make you feel like you cannot improve or that your goals are too big. It can also make you worry about what others think. In this chapter, we will look at different kinds of doubt and how to handle them in a calm and honest way.

1. **Understanding Where Doubt Comes From**
   Doubt often starts as a small thought or worry. You might think, "Am I good enough?" or "What if people do not like my work?" Sometimes, these thoughts come from a single bad experience—a failed audition or a negative comment online. Other times, they come from comparing yourself to someone more advanced. Recognizing that doubt has a source helps you see it is not some unstoppable force. It is a feeling that grows from certain triggers, and you can learn to handle it.

Doubt is also linked to fear of the unknown. When you push forward into areas where you have never been, your mind might say, "Maybe this is too hard." This feeling is normal, because your brain wants to protect you from potential failure. However, if you let it grow unchecked, it can prevent you from testing your limits or accepting new opportunities. Seeing doubt as a normal human reaction can help you greet it more calmly, rather than letting it overwhelm you.

2. **Separating Useful Doubt from Harmful Doubt**
   Not all doubt is bad. Sometimes, a little uncertainty can save you from rushing into something unwise. For example, if you doubt your readiness for a big show and decide to practice harder first, that can be helpful. This type of doubt pushes you to double-check your work or get extra training.

Harmful doubt, on the other hand, makes you feel like giving up before you even try. It becomes a roadblock instead of a guide. If you find that doubt is keeping you stuck rather than making you more careful or prepared, it is likely the harmful kind. Learning to tell the difference helps you decide when to trust your doubts and when to move past them.

3. **Identifying Your Doubt Triggers**
   A "trigger" is something that sparks a strong emotion. For example, maybe you feel a wave of doubt every time you watch a performer who is very advanced. Or perhaps it hits when someone questions your choices. By spotting these triggers, you can plan how to respond in a healthier way.

If you notice that watching big-name actors on TV makes you think you will never reach that level, you could set a limit on how often you watch them. Another option is to view them with a learning mindset instead of a comparing mindset. That shift can lessen the trigger. The key is to be aware of what sets off your doubts so you can manage the situation rather than walk into it unprepared.

4. **Talking Back to Negative Thoughts**
   When doubt appears, it often speaks in your mind with phrases like "I will fail" or "I am not talented." One way to handle these thoughts is to talk back to them in a calm and factual way. For instance, if your mind says, "I will fail," you can remind yourself of times you have succeeded or improved. If your mind says, "I am not talented," you can recall feedback from mentors or moments when your work received praise.

This does not mean you pretend to be perfect. Rather, you balance the negative voice by showing yourself realistic evidence of your strengths. Over time, this practice teaches your brain that those harsh words are not the full truth. You might even choose a short phrase to repeat, such as "I am still growing, and I have made progress," whenever you sense doubt creeping in.

5. **Seeking Honest Feedback from Trusted People**
   Doubt can grow if you keep your worries locked inside. Instead, talk to people you trust—like a friend, family member, mentor, or fellow artist.

Share what you are concerned about. Let them give you their view. Often, the people who care about you can see your true abilities more clearly than you can when you are feeling stressed. They may remind you of your achievements or point out new ways you can improve.

If you feel uncertain about a specific project, getting feedback from someone with expertise in that area can help you see whether your doubt is fair. For example, if you worry that your voice is not strong enough for a certain song, you can ask a singing teacher to evaluate your tone. If they say you need more practice on breath control, you can focus on that rather than letting vague doubts hold you back. If they say you sound ready, you can accept that good news and move forward with more confidence.

---

6. **Using Failure as a Lesson Rather Than Proof of Inadequacy**
   People often let doubt grow stronger after a mistake or failure. For instance, if you lose a contest or get turned down at an audition, you might tell yourself, "That proves I do not have what it takes." However, failure can be a teacher if you are open to learning from it. Instead of seeing it as proof that you are not good enough, ask, "What specifically went wrong, and how can I fix it next time?"

Maybe you lacked enough preparation. Maybe your choice of material did not match the style of that particular event. Identifying the real reason behind a failure can keep you from blaming yourself in a general way. Plus, it gives you a clear path to improvement. Each time you learn from a setback, you weaken the power of doubt.

---

7. **Practicing Self-Encouragement**
   Encouraging yourself might sound odd if you are used to hearing self-criticism in your mind. But just as negative words can tear you down, positive ones can build you up. You could write down a few sentences that remind you of your goals and strengths. For instance: "I am committed to growing my talent. I have unique ideas to share with others. I am allowed to learn at my own pace."

Some people stick these lines on a mirror or near their desk. Reading them daily can help retrain your thoughts. Of course, you do not want to go too far and become unrealistic, but a balance of truthful, kind words can keep doubt from running wild. This habit can be a powerful tool against the worries that pop up in your mind.

---

8. **Comparing Yourself Only to Your Past Self**

    Comparison is a major source of doubt. You might see someone else's fast success or watch their flawless performances and think, "I will never get there." But remember that everyone's path is different. The real measure of growth is whether you have improved compared to your own past, not someone else's present.

Ask yourself: "Am I better at my skill than I was last year?" or "Do I have more knowledge than before?" If the answer is yes, you are on the right track. Also, remember that you do not always see the hard parts of another person's life. They might look perfect on stage but still deal with struggles you cannot see. Focusing on your own progress reduces the chance of self-doubt fueled by unrealistic comparisons.

---

9. **Setting Achievable Steps**

    A large goal—like becoming nationally known—can feel overwhelming. That can feed doubt because you might think, "I cannot possibly reach something that big." However, if you break your goal into smaller steps, each step feels more doable. For example, you might first aim to get a certain number of local fans, then to perform at a local event, then at a regional event.

Each time you check off a small step, your confidence grows a bit, and the doubt fades. You see real proof that you can make progress. Over time, this momentum helps you aim for even bigger steps. Keeping your goals in small, clear units also ensures that you do not let your mind spin with vague fear about a huge end result.

10. **Creating a Supportive Environment**
    The people and atmosphere around you can influence your doubt levels. If you have friends who constantly mock your goals or focus on failures, your sense of self might weaken. On the other hand, if you spend time with supportive people who believe in growth and effort, their attitude can lift you up. This does not mean you must cut ties with anyone who criticizes you, but consider limiting how much weight you give to their words.

A supportive environment can also include physical spaces. Maybe you practice in a room that feels calm and organized, with reminders of your aims. Or you might listen to motivational talks or read uplifting stories before you start a new project. All these elements together can form a shield against persistent doubt.

---

11. **Knowing Doubt Is Common, Even Among Top Performers**
    It is easy to believe that famous people never doubt themselves because we see them at their best. However, many top athletes, actors, and singers admit they still feel nervous or uncertain. Some experience performance anxiety before every show but have learned to manage it. This knowledge can comfort you: doubt does not vanish when you get successful; you just get better at handling it.

Reading or listening to interviews where well-known figures talk about their insecurities can help you see that doubt is normal. If they overcame it or learned to work with it, so can you. This does not fix doubt overnight, but it can reduce the sense that you are alone or flawed for feeling uncertain.

---

12. **Learning to Accept Constructive Criticism Without Letting It Crush You**
    Constructive criticism aims to help you improve, while harsh or useless criticism simply attacks you. Distinguishing between these two types is crucial. When you get constructive comments—like someone pointing out a weak spot in your performance but giving advice to correct it—you can use it to get better. That might spark a momentary doubt, but it is based on a real gap you can fix.

Useless criticism might just be someone saying, "You are terrible, quit now." That does not provide any path to improve. It only aims to hurt. Learning to let those remarks bounce off you is essential. You can do this by calmly telling yourself, "This critic did not give me anything helpful. Their words say more about them than about me." Over time, you will become better at telling the difference and saving your energy for the feedback that helps you grow.

---

13. **Trying Different Methods to Reduce Worries**
    Sometimes, you can fight doubt by tweaking your routine. For instance, if you feel panicky before a performance, you might do some light stretching or breathing exercises. If you worry about forgetting lines, you can add an extra 15 minutes of memorization each day until you feel comfortable. If you doubt your ability to handle an interview, practice with a friend first.

Experiment with different methods. Some people like journaling their thoughts, others prefer listening to relaxing music before stepping on stage. The idea is to find a strategy that calms your mind enough so doubt does not dominate you. Each success with a new method tells your brain, "I can handle this."

---

14. **Setting Realistic Expectations**
    You might fuel your own doubt by expecting yourself to be perfect. If your idea of success is to have zero mistakes every time, you will likely be disappointed. Even the greatest performers slip up or have an off day. Setting realistic expectations—like wanting to do your best under the circumstances—helps you feel less crushed when things do not go exactly as planned.

For example, aim to learn the basics well, show steady improvement, or entertain the crowd with sincerity. Those are targets you can reach, even if you miss a note or forget a line. When you accept that small errors are part of the process, you free yourself from the fear that every slip is a disaster.

15. **Staying Patient with Slow Progress**
    Doubt can creep in when progress seems slow. You might practice a skill for months and feel like you are hardly moving forward. However, many forms of growth happen so gradually that you do not notice until you compare your performance to months or years ago. Patience can be hard in a world that often praises quick results, but patience is a big ally against doubt.

If you keep a practice log or recordings of your work, you can look back to see how far you have come. This can remind you that even slow improvements are improvements. Celebrate those small steps in your own quiet way and continue pressing on. Remember that lasting skill usually takes more time to build than short-lived skill. Patience can keep your self-belief alive through these slower phases.

---

16. **Using Visualization for Confidence**
    Visualization means imagining yourself performing well or finishing a task with skill. Some athletes use it to picture landing a perfect jump; some speakers use it to see themselves delivering clear words on stage. When you do this, try to involve your senses—imagine the lights, the sounds, the feeling of calm in your body. This mental practice can reduce the hold of doubt, because your brain becomes more comfortable with the idea of succeeding.

You can do visualization for just a few minutes each day. Find a quiet spot, close your eyes, and see yourself doing the exact moves or steps needed for your task. Combine this with actual practice so you still build real skills. Visualization does not replace hard work; it complements it by calming your mind and boosting confidence.

---

17. **Keeping a Record of Your Wins**
    When doubt tells you that you never do anything right, it is helpful to have a record of achievements that prove otherwise. You might keep a notebook or a digital file listing positive comments, awards, finished projects, or personal successes. Whenever you feel uncertain, you can

look at this record. It is not about bragging; it is about reminding yourself of your real progress.

Even small wins count, like a positive note from a teacher or a friendly message from someone who appreciated your work. By building this collection over time, you have clear evidence that you have accomplished things, which weakens the idea that you cannot succeed. This is especially useful on days when your mind tries to convince you otherwise.

---

18. **Taking Breaks When Doubt Overwhelms You**
    Sometimes, doubt can get so loud that pushing forward feels impossible in that moment. If you reach that level of stress, it might help to pause rather than force yourself to continue. Step away from practice, take a short walk, or do something you find calming. This break is not quitting; it is a way to refresh your mind so you can come back to the task with a clearer head.

During this break, do not just stew in negative thoughts. Try to shift your focus to something comforting, like a hobby or a simple activity. When you return, you might see your work differently. A rested brain often has better problem-solving ability and can see solutions that were missed before.

---

19. **Finding Motivational Stories**
    Reading or listening to stories of people who overcame strong doubt can inspire you. They might be individuals who faced rejections or personal hardships yet kept going until they found a breakthrough. These accounts can remind you that you are not alone and that doubt does not have to decide your fate.

Look for stories in books, podcasts, or documentaries. They do not have to be about the same exact field as yours. A scientist who overcame obstacles can still teach you about perseverance, even if you want to be a performer. The main point is that these examples show how a person's drive and belief can triumph over fear and setbacks.

---

20. **Limiting Oversharing Your Doubts Publicly**
    While it is good to talk to trusted friends or mentors about your fears, oversharing your doubts on public platforms can sometimes make them stronger. Some people might respond kindly, but others could exploit those worries to tear you down. Sharing everything openly might also make you dwell on negative thoughts.

Choose a safe circle (or an individual) for discussing deeper worries. Keep public discussions more centered on your work, your progress, or general insights. That way, you protect your mind from unnecessary outside negativity. You can still be honest, but in a way that does not invite unhelpful attacks when you are feeling low.

---

21. **Stepping Out of Your Comfort Zone in Small Ways**
    A good technique to handle doubt is to face it in small steps. If you are afraid of performing live, start with a tiny audience, such as a group of friends, before moving to a larger venue. If you are scared of sharing your writing, show it to one or two people before posting it online. By taking these smaller steps, you teach yourself that you can deal with a bit of discomfort. Over time, your comfort zone grows, and doubt shrinks.

It is normal to feel nervous each time you push the boundary, but each success—no matter how small—chips away at doubt. You get more used to the feeling of being challenged and realize you can survive and even thrive in new situations.

---

22. **Turning Doubt Into Curiosity**
    When you think, "I do not know if I can do this," try rephrasing it as, "I wonder if I can figure out how to do this." This small shift can turn doubt into curiosity, which is a more open-ended feeling. Curiosity leads to questions like, "What if I try a different approach?" or "Who can I ask for tips?" Instead of shutting you down, it motivates you to explore.

This mindset also makes setbacks feel like clues. If something fails, you become curious about a new path. You might ask, "Why didn't that work? What can I try next time?" That attitude can help you avoid the trap of saying, "I failed because I am not good enough." Instead, you see it as a puzzle to solve. Gradually, doubt becomes less of a block and more of a reminder to stay curious and keep learning.

---

23. **Recognizing Progress Takes Time**
    Some forms of doubt arise from impatience. You might expect quick results after a few weeks of practice or a few posts online. When that does not happen, doubt says, "This is never going to work." Remember that most successes are built over months and years, not days. If you quit too soon, you might never see the fruit of your early efforts.

When you feel frustrated, step back and remember that even the biggest names in your field likely spent a long time honing their craft before getting recognized. This is normal. Each day of effort stacks up. If you trust that process, doubt becomes less convincing when it tries to say you are behind.

---

24. **Accepting Doubt as Part of Growth**
    Instead of trying to destroy doubt completely, you can accept that it will show up whenever you stretch yourself. Each new level brings uncertainty because it is new territory. That is okay. Doubt can keep you cautious and alert. The goal is not to remove doubt but to keep it in check so it does not stop you.

By accepting it, you remove some of its power to make you afraid. You might say to yourself, "Yes, I feel uncertain, and that is normal. I can keep going anyway." With this view, doubt no longer stands as a wall but becomes a small hurdle you know how to step over or walk around. It is still there, but it is not in control.

Wrapping Up Chapter 9
Doubt can come from many places, but it does not have to hold you back from becoming well-known for your talent or skill. By recognizing triggers, seeking honest feedback, and practicing realistic thinking, you can reduce its impact. Remember that nearly everyone—famous or not—faces doubt in some form. The difference is whether you allow it to halt your progress or guide you to refine

your approach. Keep learning, keep testing your limits, and see doubt as a reminder that you are pushing yourself. When managed well, doubt can help you stay grounded while you aim high.

In the next chapter, we will discuss how to share your story online in a clear and appealing way. Putting yourself out there on the internet can open doors to a big audience, but it also comes with unique challenges. We will explore how to choose the right platform, keep your content true to who you are, and engage with viewers in a positive manner.

CHAPTER 10: SHARING YOUR STORY ONLINE

The internet has made it simpler than ever to show your talents, thoughts, and experiences to people everywhere. Even if you live in a small town or lack big-stage connections, you can post content and possibly reach viewers from across the globe. At the same time, standing out online can be tough because so many people are also sharing. In this chapter, we will look at how to share your story online in a natural way, so that people notice and remember you.

1. **Deciding Which Parts of Your Story to Share**
   Before you start posting, think about what you want people to know about you. This includes your background, your goals, and the path that led you to your current skill level. You do not have to reveal every single detail. Some personal parts of your life might remain private. The main idea is to give viewers a sense of who you are and why your work is special.

For example, you might decide to share that you grew up in a certain place where music was part of your family culture, and that this inspired you. You could discuss how you saved up for a better instrument by doing small jobs. But maybe you do not want to talk about family conflicts or deeper struggles. That is up to you. Keeping a line between personal and public information helps you stay safe and comfortable online.

2. **Picking the Right Platform**
   There are many ways to share your story. You can use video-sharing sites, social media pages, blogging platforms, or audio podcasts. Each platform has its style. If you have a strong visual element (like singing, dancing, or painting), a video platform might show your work better. If you are a writer or you want to share thoughtful pieces, a blog or text-based platform could suit you. If you like quick, short updates, a micro-blogging site might be best.

It can help to start with one main platform rather than trying to be everywhere. Focusing your efforts allows you to grow a dedicated audience. Later, you can branch out if you want. Think about where your potential fans hang out. If you are aiming to reach younger viewers, certain platforms might be more popular. If you want a more professional crowd, choose a site known for business or skill-based discussions.

3. **Creating a Clear Online Profile**
   Your profile is often the first thing people see. It should quickly tell them what you do and what they can expect from you. Use a photo that looks friendly or matches your style. Write a short description that includes your main skill, your interest, or a short phrase that captures your focus. For instance, "Singer and songwriter sharing heartfelt tunes," or "Sports trainer with tips for simple home workouts."

A consistent profile picture or logo across platforms can help people recognize you if they find you in multiple places. You might also use the same color scheme or style in your banners, thumbnails, or posts. This visual unity helps you look professional and makes it easier for viewers to remember your online presence.

4. **Telling Your Story Step by Step**
   Sharing your background can be done over time, instead of in one big post. This approach keeps people interested. You could start with a brief introduction—"Hello, I am [Name], and here is why I love this art form"—then later share smaller pieces like how you practiced as a beginner, the funny challenges you faced, or any inspiring role models you looked up to.

By spreading out these story pieces, you give viewers a chance to get to know you bit by bit. They might come back to see what happens next. This also lets you add fresh details and keep the narrative going without overwhelming people with a huge life story in one go.

5. **Using Authenticity to Connect**
   Authenticity means being real. Viewers can often tell when someone is faking a style or forcing a personality that is not theirs. If you speak about

your experiences or feelings in an honest way (without oversharing private matters), people are more likely to trust you. For example, if you are nervous about trying a new skill, you can mention that. This can make others say, "Hey, I feel that way too!"

You do not have to be dramatic for the sake of clicks. Simply share moments that shaped who you are, the obstacles you tackled, and the joy you find in what you do. Authenticity can be as simple as talking in your normal voice, writing like you speak in daily life, or showing how you practice in a real setting instead of a carefully staged environment all the time.

---

6. **Mixing Content: Skill Showcases and Personal Insights**
   If you only post about your private life, people might not see your talent clearly. If you only post skill-based content, people might not feel a personal connection. A good balance is to mix these in a natural way. Show a clip of you working on your talent—singing a verse of your new song or demonstrating a quick tutorial for your art technique—then sometimes share a reflection on what you learned that day or what motivated you to try something new.

These personal insights can be short. A simple "Today, I struggled with X, but it helped me see Y" can let people connect with the real person behind the talent. Over time, viewers who come for the skill might stay because they appreciate your thoughts and experiences.

---

7. **Using Simple, Friendly Language**
   Whether you post videos, write blogs, or record podcasts, keep your words clear and direct. You do not need fancy phrases to stand out. In fact, using simple language often attracts more people, because they can follow your message without confusion. Remember that your audience might include people from various backgrounds, ages, or places around the world.

If you are explaining a process (like how to record a song at home), break it down into easy steps. If you are telling a story, keep it flowing in a way that someone with no background knowledge can follow. That sense of clarity makes your content inviting and easy to share.

8. **Sharing the Ups and the Downs**
   People appreciate seeing the real ups and downs of someone's path, not just a highlight reel. Of course, you might want to show your best side when presenting your skill, but including some honest talk about the rough spots can build trust. Maybe you had a time when no one was watching your videos, or you got poor feedback at a local contest. Sharing how you coped can bring you closer to your followers.

However, keep it balanced. If all you share is bad news or frustrations, people might feel tired or gloomy when they see your updates. Show them that tough times can lead to lessons or new approaches. If you remain genuine and balanced, viewers will appreciate your honesty and the hope that goes with it.

9. **Involving Your Audience**
   One way to grow a loyal following is to let your viewers or readers participate in some way. This could be something small like asking for song suggestions or new challenge ideas. You might say, "What should I paint next?" or "Which topic do you want me to cover in my next post?" This involvement makes people feel part of your creative process.

You can also hold Q&A sessions. Let your audience send questions about your work or your background. Answer them in a video or a post. This direct contact can turn casual watchers into supportive fans. They feel seen and heard, and you learn more about what they find interesting.

10. **Staying Consistent with Posting**
    Once you start sharing, aim for a schedule that you can keep. It does not have to be daily—maybe once a week or once every two weeks is fine—but be regular enough that people know when to expect new content. Consistency shows you are serious about your craft and your online

presence. It also helps you maintain momentum. If you vanish for months without explaining, some followers might drift away.

Planning your content ahead of time can prevent last-minute stress. You could outline the topics or performances for the next few posts or videos. This does not mean you have to stick to a rigid plan if you get a fresh idea, but having a structure helps you stay focused. It also helps avoid gaps that might cause you to scramble for material.

---

11. **Engaging with Comments or Feedback**
    If people comment on your posts—whether they praise you or have questions—try to respond, especially at the start when your audience is smaller. A simple reply like, "Thank you, I appreciate it," or "That is a great suggestion, I will try it," can encourage more interaction next time. As you grow, you might not manage to reply to everyone, but showing you care about the conversation can make a big difference.

Also, be ready to see negative comments. Some might be rude or unhelpful, which you can ignore or remove if they break the rules you set. Others might offer constructive points or ask questions that sound harsh but could help you improve. Use your judgment to decide which comments merit a thoughtful reply and which are just meant to offend.

---

12. **Joining Online Communities and Groups**
    Apart from posting on your own profile, you can connect with others in your field. Look for groups or forums where people with similar interests gather. For instance, if you do digital art, there might be communities where artists share tips or challenges. Take part in discussions, offer advice, and post your own work when relevant.

Being active in groups lets you show your knowledge and personality, which can attract people to your own pages. However, do not just spam your content everywhere. Focus on adding real value, like offering kind feedback to others or asking insightful questions. This approach builds a good reputation and helps you stand out in a positive way.

13. **Collaborating with Other Creators**
    One effective strategy for building an online audience is collaborating with others who have a similar or related focus. For example, if you are a singer, you might team up with someone who plays an instrument. If you are a cook, you could partner with a baker. You could do a shared video or a co-hosted live stream, so each partner introduces the other to their fans.

This helps both parties tap into new audiences. Plus, seeing two creators work together can be fun and fresh for viewers. When planning a collaboration, make sure you pick someone whose style or values match yours. That way, the final product feels natural, and both sets of followers enjoy the mix.

---

14. **Telling Stories Through Photos or Short Clips**
    Not all storytelling needs to be long. Sometimes, a single photo or a 30-second clip can reveal a lot about you. You might show your workspace, a snippet of your warm-up routine, or a snapshot of an event you are attending. Add a short caption that provides context: "Practicing my new riff," or "Getting ready for my first local gallery show." These quick peeks into your day-to-day can create a sense of closeness with viewers who want to see behind the scenes.

Short clips also tend to do well on social media, where people's attention might be brief. If they like your short post, they might then seek out your longer videos or full blog to learn more. In that sense, short content can act as a friendly "hello" that leads people to your deeper material.

---

15. **Handling Online Criticism or Drama**
    The internet has its share of arguments and toxic behavior. If someone tries to pull you into a hostile argument, pause and think: "Is this discussion useful or is it a fight that will waste my energy?" You can choose to step away from arguments that have no clear benefit. If you do respond, keep it calm and respectful. Do not let others provoke you into saying things you might regret.

If criticism is directed at your personal story, remember that not everyone will understand your background or choices. You can clarify if you wish. But if the person seems to be attacking for no reason, it is often best to focus on people who appreciate your work or give fair, honest feedback. No one can please the entire internet.

---

16. **Using Hashtags or Keywords Wisely**
    When posting, think about which tags or words can help people find you. For example, if you are a makeup artist, using relevant tags like #makeuptips or #beautybasics might draw viewers who are interested in that topic. However, do not overload your post with too many tags. That can seem spammy and might even turn people away.

A few specific tags can connect you with the right group of viewers. Over time, you can learn which tags bring more engagement. Each platform has its norms for how many tags are acceptable. Observe what other successful creators in your niche are doing, and adapt their methods to fit your style.

---

17. **Telling a Consistent Story Over Time**
    When sharing your story, keep a sense of continuity. If one day you say you started singing at age 5 because your family was musical, and another day you say you only found music in high school, viewers might become confused. That does not mean you cannot reveal new details. Just be sure not to contradict what you said before.

It can help to keep a simple timeline or bullet points about key moments in your background. This way, if you do a Q&A and someone asks about your early inspirations, you can repeat the facts you have shared before. Consistency builds trust. People know they can rely on what you say and are more likely to support you as a result.

---

18. **Avoiding Over-Editing the Truth**
    It is good to present your best side, but if you edit your life too much, you might look like a completely different person online. That might draw

attention for a while, but it can be draining to maintain an image that is far from who you are. If you are known for being bright and energetic online but are naturally quiet in real life, you might find it hard to keep up the loud persona at live events or interviews.

Aim for a realistic level of polish. Clean up your photos or videos if you like, but let your real face and style show. Trim your words if needed, but let your real voice come through. This honesty will attract an audience that likes you for who you are.

---

19. **Sharing Skills or Tutorials**

    One way to show your expertise is by teaching bits of it. If you are a dancer, you might share a simple move that beginners can try. If you are a writer, maybe you post a tip about plotting a story or picking the right words. Teaching helps viewers see that you know your field. It also gives them value, which makes them more likely to follow or subscribe.

You do not have to give away all your secrets. Just a few short lessons or tips can pique interest. Plus, teaching often strengthens your own understanding. You might discover new insights as you think about how to explain things simply. This approach can grow an audience that respects your knowledge and becomes eager for your bigger projects.

---

20. **Staying Aware of Safety**

    While sharing your story online can bring good connections, be mindful of what you make public. Avoid posting addresses or routines that could put you at risk. For example, you might not want to share your exact daily schedule or reveal where you live. If you get invitations from strangers to meet, consider the safety concerns before saying yes. Check if it is in a public place or if you should bring a friend.

Also, be careful with links or files from people you do not know well. They can contain harmful software. Keep an eye on your privacy settings so you know who can see your posts. If you find someone behaving strangely or sending you uncomfortable messages, block them or report them to the platform if needed.

21. **Learning Basic Tech Skills**
    You do not have to be a computer expert, but knowing some basics can help you share your story smoothly. For example, learn how to film a clear video or record decent audio. If you write a blog, learn how to format text so it is easy to read. Small details—like good lighting, readable fonts, or clear sound—can raise the quality of your presentation and keep visitors interested.

If you struggle with tech stuff, you can find free online guides or ask a friend to show you the ropes. Over time, the basic skills become second nature, and you will be able to focus more on the actual content you are sharing.

22. **Balancing Promotion with Connection**
    While it is important to promote your work, too much promotion can push people away. Nobody wants every post to be "Buy my product" or "Watch my video now!" Involve people in your process instead. Show how you are making the new song, mention interesting facts, or ask for opinions on cover designs. This kind of content feels more engaging and less like a direct sales pitch.

When you do share a finished product or event, do it in a friendly way: "I am excited to post my new track today. I hope you enjoy it. Let me know what you think!" Then, continue normal posts with insights or skill-building. This variety keeps your audience from feeling that you only see them as potential buyers or numbers.

23. **Gathering Data and Adapting**
    Most online platforms show statistics, like how many people watched your video or how many clicked "like." Check these stats to see what kind of content resonates most. For example, you might discover that your short behind-the-scenes clips get double the views compared to your long sit-down discussions. This does not mean you have to give up longer content, but it can guide how you plan your future posts.

Also, pay attention to comments or direct messages asking for more of a certain type of content. If people say they love your short comedic skits, maybe lean more in that direction or blend it with your main talent. Staying flexible while still remaining true to your overall style can help your online presence grow naturally.

---

24. **Growing at Your Own Pace**
    Some creators go viral overnight, but many build an audience slowly over months or years. Do not feel discouraged if your follower count does not explode immediately. Each person who finds your page and connects with your story is a real person. If you treat them well and keep offering good content, word of mouth can bring more people over time.

Enjoy the process of putting your work and your personal story out there. Overthinking numbers can cause stress. Instead, keep focusing on quality, authenticity, and steady improvement. As you refine your approach based on honest feedback, your online presence can become a powerful way to share who you are and what you do best.

Wrapping Up Chapter 10
Sharing your story online is one of the most accessible routes to recognition. By choosing the right platform, crafting a clear profile, and balancing skill-focused posts with personal reflections, you can form real connections. People want to feel like they know the person behind the talent. Once trust is built, they often become loyal supporters who will cheer you on and tell others about you.

Keep your safety and well-being in mind as you open up pieces of your life to the public. Stay aware that not everyone will be kind, but many will offer genuine praise or friendly suggestions. With patience and consistency, your online presence can grow into a strong stage that helps you advance on the path to being widely recognized. In the next chapters, we will look at how to use traditional media, such as newspapers and radio, and how to find the right audience for your style of work. By combining online reach with other forms of publicity, you can broaden your impact while staying true to yourself.

CHAPTER 11: USING TRADITIONAL MEDIA

Modern technology gives people easy ways to share their work online, yet traditional media—like newspapers, magazines, radio, and TV—still holds power. Getting a feature in your local newspaper or an interview on a local station can open doors to a different set of viewers, many of whom may not spend as much time on social platforms. Traditional media can also give you a certain level of legitimacy, since these outlets have been around for many years and often have established trust in their communities. In this chapter, we will look at how to connect with traditional media outlets and make the most of the opportunities they can offer.

1. **Why Traditional Media Still Matters**
   It is easy to think that everyone uses the internet for their news, entertainment, or stories. But many people still rely on TV news, radio shows during car rides, or a local paper's weekend section for local events and profiles of interesting people. For instance, older audiences, or those in certain communities, may have stronger ties to these outlets. Also, traditional outlets often have dedicated reporters or producers with a strong sense of what their local public wants.

Another reason to care about these outlets is that they can place you next to recognized names. If your local paper covers well-known city events, or if your regional radio station interviews both big performers and rising ones, being included there can position you as part of a respected group. You might get invited to bigger opportunities down the road if someone notices your feature in a newspaper or sees you on a local TV segment.

2. **Understanding Different Types of Traditional Media**
   Traditional media comes in several forms:
   - **Newspapers**: These can be daily, weekly, or monthly, and some focus on local stories, while others have a broader scope.
   - **Magazines**: These often revolve around a particular topic, such as lifestyle, arts, sports, or culture.

- **Radio**: Stations might cover news, talk shows, music segments, or community happenings.
- **TV**: Local stations may run morning news, community interest segments, or late-night features.

Each type has its own style and audience. For example, a daily newspaper might want short, timely items about new events or achievements, while a monthly magazine might prefer longer interviews and in-depth stories. A morning radio show might enjoy brief, lively interviews, whereas a community radio hour could allow a more detailed conversation. Knowing these nuances helps you figure out where to focus your energy.

3. **Identifying the Right Outlets for Your Field**
   Instead of sending emails to every possible station or publication, you can narrow down the best fit. Look at local newspapers that have sections for arts, sports, business, or human-interest stories. If you are a musician, find a publication that regularly covers local bands or music festivals. If you are an athlete, contact radio shows that highlight local sports. If you are an artist or writer, check for cultural magazines in your area that enjoy featuring new creators.

Spend some time reading or listening to the outlet you want to approach. See what tone they use—serious, fun, casual, or formal. If you match their style, your chance of getting featured could be higher. Also, if you see that they often highlight short "person of the week" pieces, you might prepare a quick summary of yourself that suits that format. If they do in-depth interviews, you might be ready for deeper questions about your background and achievements.

4. **Making a Simple Media Kit**
   A media kit is a small set of materials that explain who you are and what you do. It can include:
- **A short bio**: In a paragraph or two, explain your background, your main field, and any important milestones.
- **High-quality pictures**: These could be headshots, pictures of you performing, or images of your art. Make sure they are clear and well-lit. Outlets may want to use them in print or on their website.

- **Contact details**: Include an email address and possibly a phone number. If you have a personal website or social profile with more info, include links.
- **Any notable achievements**: If you have won small awards, performed in known venues, or done collaborations with recognized people, mention them.

This kit helps reporters or producers quickly learn about you without digging around. It shows that you are prepared and serious about being featured. You do not need a fancy design—just keep it neat and easy to read.

---

5. **Crafting a Press Release**

   A press release is a short document that announces news about you. It can be sent to newspapers, radio stations, or magazines. Usually, a press release has:

- **A clear headline**: Something like "Local Singer Releases Debut Album with a Personal Touch" or "Teen Athlete Sets New Record in Community Contest."
- **A quick summary**: One or two sentences that give the most important details.
- **Main body**: A few paragraphs with background on who you are, why this news matters, where people can learn more, and any quotes from you or someone else involved.
- **Contact info**: So they can reach you for further questions or an interview.

If you have a new show, a book release, an art exhibit, or any specific event, you can write a short press release and send it to relevant outlets. Keep it factual and clear. Reporters get many releases each day, so you want yours to stand out by being direct, interesting, and free of hype. If there is a local angle—like how your event ties into a community cause—highlight that, because local outlets often want stories that link to their region.

---

6. **Approaching Journalists and Editors Politely**

   When you have identified potential outlets and gathered your materials, the next step is reaching out. Email is common, though some smaller outlets might also respond to phone calls. Your message should briefly say who you are, why you are contacting them, and why their readers or listeners might care about your story. You can attach your press release or a link to your media kit.

Keep the tone polite and not pushy. For instance, start with "Hello, my name is [Name]. I am a [your field] from [area]. I noticed your publication often covers local arts, and I thought you might be interested in my upcoming show." Then give a short summary of what is special or newsworthy about you. Provide a link or attachment to your press release for more details.

If you do not hear back, you can send one polite follow-up note after a week or two. But do not flood their inbox. If they are not interested at this time, forcing the issue usually does not help. You can try again later with fresh news or after you have gained more experience.

7. **Preparing for an Interview**

   If a reporter, host, or editor shows interest, you might be asked for an interview. This could be a quick phone call, an on-air radio spot, or a formal sit-down for a newspaper piece. It is natural to feel nervous. Here are some tips:
   - **Know your main talking points**: Think about the key facts you want people to remember—who you are, what you do, and why it matters.
   - **Rehearse brief answers**: Journalists might ask about your background or your project. Practice short, clear replies that hit the main points.
   - **Stay relaxed and friendly**: Speak at a moderate pace. If it is a live interview, it is okay to pause and gather your thoughts. Try to answer questions calmly.
   - **Offer examples or anecdotes**: If you can share a short story that illustrates your work, that can be more memorable than vague statements.
   - **Double-check details**: If there is a show date or a website, mention it clearly so the interviewer can pass that info on to the audience.

Remember, an interview is not just about you talking—it is also about helping the reporter get a story that hooks their readers or viewers. Offer interesting angles or personal insights so they have strong material to use.

8. **Handling Radio and TV Spots**
   Radio and TV appearances can be especially valuable because they let people hear your voice or see you in action. However, they can also feel nerve-racking if you have never done it before. Keep these pointers in mind:
   - **Arrive early**: If it is an in-person studio interview, you might need time to park, sign in, and get set up. If you are doing a remote interview by phone or video, be ready at least ten minutes beforehand.
   - **Dress appropriately**: For radio, it might not matter as much, but it is still good to feel neat and confident. For TV, choose something that looks nice on camera—avoid super bright or busy patterns if you can.
   - **Speak clearly**: Even if you are excited, try not to rush. Enunciate your words so the audience can follow.
   - **Look at the host (for TV)**: If you are on a set, focus on the host or the person you are talking to, rather than staring at the camera.
   - **Show positivity**: Even if you are serious about your topic, having a warm, upbeat tone can engage viewers and listeners.

Radio and TV segments can sometimes be short—maybe just a few minutes. Try to make the most of that time by hitting your main message and letting your personality shine.

---

9. **Working with Photographers or Camera Crews**
   If a local paper or TV station sends someone to take pictures or record video, approach it as a chance to give them something visually appealing. For instance, if you are a dancer, you might show them a few moves rather than just standing still. If you are an artist, let them film you painting or sketching. Action shots can make the feature more interesting for the audience.

If you feel awkward with a camera pointing at you, focus on your skill. Do the activity you do best, and try to forget the camera is there. The photographer or camera person is used to capturing genuine moments, so let them do their job. You can also offer suggestions like, "I can play a short section of my new song, if that helps." This kind of cooperation can yield better results and a more engaging article or clip.

10. **Being Grateful and Building Relationships**
    When a newspaper publishes a piece about you or a radio show invites you, it is a big deal. Even if you do not see immediate huge results, it can still help your name reach people who might not have heard of you before. Send a short thank-you note or email to the reporter or producer who worked with you. Let them know you appreciate their time and the coverage.

Building goodwill can lead to future mentions. For example, if you have a major update a few months later—like releasing a follow-up project—you can gently reach out to that same contact, reminding them of the last piece they did. They might be willing to feature you again. Positive, respectful communication leaves a good impression and can turn a one-time interview into an ongoing media connection.

---

11. **Handling Tough or Unexpected Questions**
    Sometimes, interviews do not go as smoothly as you hope. A reporter might ask something that catches you off guard, like a sensitive detail about your life or a controversy in your field. If you are uncomfortable with the question, you can give a brief, polite response that does not reveal more than you want. For example, "I prefer to keep that part private, but I can say…" and then steer the topic back to your work.

If the question is about a broader issue you are not prepared to discuss, it is acceptable to say you do not have enough info at the moment. Avoid getting defensive. Stay calm and try not to show anger or fear. Most interviews will be polite and supportive, but if you ever face a tricky moment, your composure is what people remember most.

---

12. **Following Up and Sharing the Coverage**
    Once your piece airs or is printed, share it with your audience. Link to the online article, or take a photo of the printed page (if that is allowed) and post it on your social pages, saying something like, "Thank you to [Outlet Name] for featuring me!" This not only shows respect to the outlet but also encourages your supporters to check out the coverage. It can lead to

more clicks or readers for the publication, which makes them see you as a helpful partner.

If you have a website, consider adding a "Press" or "News" section where you list or link to any articles, interviews, or TV clips. Over time, this can serve as proof of your growing recognition. It also provides an easy reference for other media folks who might be deciding whether to feature you. They can see you have been covered before and are a reliable subject.

---

13. **Staying Professional Over Time**
    Some people make a good impression the first time but then fade away. If you want to keep using traditional media in your climb to fame, stay professional in every interaction. Answer emails promptly. Be polite with each staff member you encounter, from the receptionist to the head producer. People in media often talk to each other; if they hear you are friendly and easy to work with, you might get more invites.

Professionalism also means being honest. If you said you would send a quote or a photo by a certain date, do it. If there is a delay, let them know. Do not exaggerate your achievements, because outlets can often fact-check. Being truthful and timely can shape your reputation as someone worthy of coverage in the future.

---

14. **Making the Most of Small Local Outlets**
    Large newspapers or big-city TV channels can be hard to reach at the start. But small outlets in your town or region may be eager for new talent to feature. They might need content to fill sections about local people who are doing something interesting. An interview in a smaller paper can still lead to new opportunities. Sometimes, bigger outlets look to smaller ones for ideas.

Do not think that a small station is a waste of time. You never know who is reading or watching. A local official or a well-known figure in your industry might see it, like what they learn about you, and invite you to a bigger opportunity. Also, it is good practice for more high-pressure interviews later. You can sharpen your talking points and learn from any mistakes when the audience is smaller.

15. **Helping Media Outlets with a Fresh Angle**
    Reporters and editors often look for a fresh angle—something that sets your story apart. Instead of saying, "I am a singer like everyone else," think about what makes you different. Maybe you learned to sing while doing chores in a busy household. Maybe you combine two unexpected styles of music. Maybe you overcame a particular challenge to get where you are. By offering a unique angle, you catch the media's interest.

Your fresh angle could also tie into a bigger topic. For instance, if the community is paying attention to a local festival, you might mention how your performance connects to that festival's theme. If a holiday is coming, you might have a special show or art piece related to it. By linking your story to what is already on people's minds, you make it easier for a media outlet to say, "Yes, that fits our schedule right now."

---

16. **Understanding the Timeline of Media Coverage**
    Traditional media often plans stories well in advance. If you want a newspaper to cover your event, contact them a few weeks (or even a couple of months) before the date. Radio shows might schedule guests several weeks ahead. Magazines, especially monthly ones, plan issues far in advance—sometimes three to six months before release.

This means you should not wait until the last minute. If your show is in three days, it might be too late for the weekly paper to fit you in. Plan your media outreach early enough that they have time to see if your news fits their schedule. Also, some outlets have deadlines for each week or month. If you know those deadlines, you can send your press release at a good time when they are planning future segments or articles.

---

17. **Handling Nerves About Public Scrutiny**
    Traditional media can feel bigger than online posts, because your words or images might appear in print or on a local channel that neighbors and acquaintances watch. This can lead to nerves about how you come across. Remember that the reporters or hosts invited you because they find your story interesting. They are generally not out to harm you. Be honest and let your real self show.

If you do worry about looking awkward on camera, practice in front of a mirror or ask a friend to do a pretend interview. Try to speak at a calm pace, keep your posture straight, and use friendly expressions. Over time, you will get more comfortable with these situations. Also, if you make a small slip or forget a word, it is not the end of the world. People often like seeing a genuine human moment.

---

18. **Handling Criticism After an Article or Segment**
    Once your piece is out, someone might say they did not like your performance or that you sounded nervous in a radio interview. This is part of public exposure. You can remind yourself that not everyone will enjoy your style or viewpoint. If the criticism seems unfair or mean, it might be best to let it pass. If it points out a real issue, like needing clearer answers or stronger stage presence, you can use that as feedback for improvement.

Stay courteous if someone contacts you directly with negative feedback. A short, calm reply can show you respect their right to an opinion. Do not start a public argument or blame the media outlet. Focus on learning and moving forward. If the coverage had any mistakes, you can politely ask the outlet to correct them. Otherwise, keep building your skill and your presence. One piece of negative feedback does not negate the value of the publicity overall.

---

19. **Turning Media Appearances into Community Engagement**
    Sometimes, a feature in local media can connect you with community events or local groups. If someone from a charity or club sees your interview, they might invite you to speak or perform. Consider saying yes if it fits your goals and schedule. Showing up at local gatherings or helping out with community projects can strengthen your reputation. It also allows you to meet people who can share more opportunities with you.

Local media loves to highlight individuals who give back or participate in local happenings. So if you do sign up for a community event, that can lead to more coverage in the future. This approach is not about seeking fame in a pushy way; it is about building real ties in your community, which in turn can raise your visibility in a natural manner.

20. **Learning from Each Appearance to Improve Next Time**
    Every interview or feature is a learning opportunity. After it happens, think about what went well and what felt awkward. Did you speak too quickly? Did you forget to mention a key detail about your upcoming event? Were you comfortable with the way you told your story? Reflecting on these points helps you do better next time.

You can also watch or read the final piece if it is publicly available. Notice how the outlet edited your words. Sometimes, they might remove parts for length. Other times, they might focus on a certain angle you mentioned. This teaches you how your story might be shaped by external editors. You can adapt your future pitches to make it easier for them to capture the heart of your work.

21. **Combining Traditional and Online Media Efforts**
    Traditional and digital approaches do not have to compete. They can support each other. If you have a good online presence, you can mention that in your interviews, directing readers or viewers to your website or social profiles for more info. If you have a strong interview in a local paper, you can share the link online and encourage your digital followers to read it. Some might then check out the newspaper's website, boosting traffic for the outlet as well.

This cross-promotion helps build a wider network. People who find you through traditional media might follow you on social platforms, and those who know you online might be interested in your local newspaper feature. Over time, the two audiences can blend, making your name recognizable in multiple circles.

22. **Respecting the Outlet's Format and Standards**
    Media outlets have rules and guidelines. For instance, certain magazines do not allow certain kinds of language. A morning TV show might want family-friendly content. A newspaper might have space limits that restrict how many words they can use. Respecting these limits and preferences increases your chances of being featured.

If you try to force them to print something that does not fit or if you keep pushing beyond deadlines, you could hurt your relationship with the editors.

Instead, show you are flexible and willing to meet them halfway. Offer a summary that fits their space if they say they can only run 250 words, for example. That willingness to adapt makes things smoother for the media professionals and makes them more likely to work with you again.

23. **Keeping Track of Your Coverage**
    Over time, you might gather several newspaper articles, radio interviews, or TV clips. Keep them organized. You could store digital versions in a folder on your computer or keep physical copies in a binder. This helps you track your progress and also makes it easier to show future outlets that you have been featured before.

Sometimes, big opportunities arise, and a producer might ask, "Have you been covered anywhere else?" You can then send them a concise list or a link to your "Press" page on your site. This demonstrates you are not a newcomer to public attention, which might give them more confidence in you as a reliable subject.

24. **Moving Forward with Confidence**
    Using traditional media well can open doors that purely online methods might not. It connects you with local communities, adds credibility to your name, and can lead to valuable networking. Remember that it is a process: you might start small, gain experience, and then aim for bigger features. Each step is a building block toward wider recognition.

Also, do not lose heart if some outlets turn you down or do not respond. That is normal. Media people have many pitches coming their way, and they cannot cover everyone. Keep refining your approach, building your track record, and developing your craft. Eventually, as your name grows and your story evolves, more outlets will see the value in sharing what you do. Traditional media can then become a steady part of your strategy for greater visibility.

Wrapping Up Chapter 11
Traditional media—newspapers, magazines, radio, and TV—still reaches broad audiences and offers a sense of recognition that can help boost your status. By

preparing a simple media kit, crafting a clear press release, and approaching journalists politely, you can stand out from the many people competing for coverage. Once you land an interview or feature, make the most of it by being ready, staying friendly, and following up with gratitude.

These appearances can build momentum, but they are just one piece of the puzzle. In the next chapter, we will talk about how to reach the right audience for your specific talent or field. You do not want your message going to people who have no interest in what you do. Instead, you want to focus on the groups most likely to appreciate and support your work. We will explore ways to identify them and make sure you tailor your efforts so that your craft resonates with those who can truly connect with it.

CHAPTER 12: REACHING THE RIGHT AUDIENCE

Becoming widely recognized is not just about getting in front of as many faces as possible—it is about getting in front of the right faces. If you make music for a certain age group, releasing it in spaces mostly used by a completely different group might not help you grow. If your content is serious, putting it on a platform known for light humor might not bring the results you want. This is why identifying and reaching the right audience is so important. In this chapter, we will look at ways to find the people who will genuinely care about your work and support you.

---

1. **Understanding What "Right Audience" Means**
   Your right audience is the group of people who find value, enjoyment, or interest in what you do. They are the ones more likely to listen to your songs if you are a musician, read your stories if you are a writer, or attend your matches if you are an athlete. They do not have to be the biggest group in the world, but they are the folks who truly connect with your style or message. They might share your material with their friends, give you constructive feedback, and cheer for you as you grow.

Sometimes, people make the mistake of trying to please everyone. This often leads to watered-down content that does not truly excite anyone. Focusing on a target group does not mean you ignore others. It simply means you place your main effort where it has the best chance of success. If your main audience is teenagers who like upbeat music, you can still welcome older listeners, but your core strategy will keep teens in mind.

---

2. **Looking at Your Current Supporters**
   A good way to identify your audience is to start with the people who already follow you or show interest. Maybe you have social media data that tells you the average age of your followers, or you can see where they live. If you are active offline, think about who comes to your events. Is it mostly families? Young adults? People in a certain career field?

Ask them questions when possible. For example, on a social page, you could post: "What made you follow my work?" or "Which of my songs do you enjoy most?" This can reveal the tastes and backgrounds of those who support you. If you discover that many are in college and enjoy a certain style, you can lean on that knowledge when planning your next steps. Or if you find a big group of fans from another country, you might think about content that includes subtle references they appreciate.

3. **Studying the Audience of Similar Creators**
   Look at successful people in your field who share something in common with you, such as genre, tone, or subject matter. Notice who follows them. Do they have a big local crowd, or does their fan base spread across different places? Are they popular with teens, professionals, or families? How do they interact with that crowd?

You can also check the comments or public groups around those creators. This gives clues about what those fans enjoy. Maybe you see that many fans talk about wanting deep lyrics or an inspiring message. Or maybe they love comedic twists. By understanding what that audience values in a similar creator, you can shape your own approach to appeal to the same kind of people—though in your unique style.

4. **Thinking About Demographics and Beyond**
   Demographics are basic facts like age, location, gender, or income level. They can be useful, but remember that real audiences are more than just a set of numbers. People also have interests, values, and personal experiences. Two people who are both 25 years old can have very different tastes. So, while demographics can help you narrow down where to look, you should also consider "psychographics"—the interests, habits, and personalities of your listeners or viewers.

For instance, if you are a chef who shares cooking tutorials, you might focus on busy parents who need quick meals. That might be an interest-based group, not just an age group. They might range from 25 to 45, but their common link is needing easy, budget-friendly recipes. By understanding that, you can craft your content to meet their needs specifically, rather than just saying, "My audience is adults."

5. **Choosing Platforms Where Your Audience Already Spends Time**
   Once you have a sense of who might be drawn to your content, you want to place your work where they are likely to be. This might mean a certain social media app, a forum, or even an offline location. For instance, if you create content for business professionals, you could focus on a platform known for professional networking or publish in business magazines. If your audience is teen gamers, you might use a platform popular for streaming game sessions or short, funny videos.

Placing your material in front of the right eyes also means you do not waste energy on places that yield little interest. Of course, you can experiment in different spots at first, but once you see a pattern—for example, that you get more engagement on a certain site—lean into that site more. Over time, you can refine your presence to focus on the spaces that truly matter.

6. **Aligning Your Style with Your Audience's Preferences**
   If you want to reach a group that values a calm, thoughtful vibe, your loud or flashy approach might scare them away. On the other hand, if your main group loves energetic, upbeat content, you might lose them with a too-quiet or serious style. That does not mean changing who you are, but you do need to present your natural personality in a manner that fits your audience.

For example, let us say you are a public speaker who talks about healthy living. If your main crowd is older people looking for calm advice, you might use a gentle voice and share simple step-by-step guidelines. If you aim for young college students seeking quick tips, you might inject humor and keep things moving fast. Both approaches can be honest to you, but they adapt to the preferences of the people you are trying to reach.

7. **Creating Content That Answers Their Needs**
   People usually pay attention to things that solve a problem or bring them joy. Ask yourself what your audience might be looking for. Does your music help them relax after a stressful day? Does your comedy lighten their mood? Does your writing offer an escape from daily worries? If you figure out what your audience is seeking, you can frame your work around that.

Even if you are doing purely creative work, you can still think about how it affects others. For example, if you paint bright, colorful pieces, you might highlight how they bring positive energy to a space. If you do stand-up comedy, you might mention that your jokes are perfect for people who want a break from routine. By linking your content to the benefits it brings, you show your audience that you understand and care about what they need.

8. **Tailoring Your Messaging**
   When you talk about your work—whether in a social post, a press release, or during an event—use words that will connect with the group you aim to attract. If your audience loves a certain slang or enjoys references to popular culture, you can sprinkle that in if it feels natural to you. If they prefer a more straightforward tone, keep it clear and direct. The way you describe your craft can either attract or repel the very people you want.

For example, if you are a guitarist focusing on classic rock, older fans might relate to references about legendary rock tours or vinyl records, while younger fans might need you to explain or show how classic rock influenced modern sounds. Adapting how you talk about it helps each group see why your work is special and relevant to them. Just be sure you do not fake knowledge or interest. People can spot dishonesty quickly, and that damages trust.

9. **Hosting Events or Activities Targeted to Your Niche**
   If your audience is local, you can set up small shows or workshops that directly cater to them. For instance, if you are an artist specializing in a style that kids enjoy, you might hold a drawing session at a community center. If your music is popular with college students, you could aim to

perform in campus events or local clubs near universities. Tailoring events to places your audience visits makes it easier for them to find you.

For online settings, you can hold live streams or Q&A sessions at times that your core group is active. If you notice that most of your fans are online in the evening, schedule your live sessions then. If they are in a certain time zone, adjust your timing so they can join comfortably. This small detail can improve attendance and help you form a stronger bond with the group.

---

10. **Collecting and Using Feedback**

    Once you start creating for your chosen group, pay attention to their responses. If you see a lot of positive reactions, that is a sign you are on the right path. If the reaction is lukewarm, it could mean that you have not quite touched on what they want. Look at comments, direct messages, or even polls. Ask for opinions: "Did this talk help you?" or "Which part of the show was your favorite?" This lets your fans guide you toward content they want more of.

Keep in mind that some feedback might be negative or harsh. Try to separate mean-spirited comments from constructive points. Mean comments might just be from someone who does not fit your target group at all. Constructive points could tell you that your videos are too long or that your writing is hard to read on mobile devices. Use that info to fine-tune your approach.

---

11. **Avoiding the Trap of Copying Competitors**

    When you see another creator in your space gaining a lot of attention, it can be tempting to copy their approach exactly. But that can lead to confusion about your identity. Also, the audience might sense you are just trying to replicate someone else. It is better to learn from others—notice what works for them—but still keep your unique style. People are drawn to authenticity. If you have a special angle or personal story, let that shine.

Imagine two chefs offering cooking videos for busy parents. One might focus on quick meals using a microwave, while the other focuses on slightly more advanced techniques but in under 20 minutes. Both can succeed if they stay true to their approach. If one chef abandons their style to mimic the other, they risk losing the distinct value they originally brought to the table.

12. **Building a Community Feeling**
    The strongest audiences feel like they are part of a community around your work. Encourage that by interacting regularly, asking them to share their experiences, and even spotlighting some of their contributions. For instance, if someone uses your method to create their own art piece or if they cover your song, share it (with their permission, of course). This kind of interaction makes them feel valued, and it shows others that you respect your fans.

Communities often form around shared passions. If you position yourself as the friendly center of that passion, people might stick around not just for your content but also for each other. This can lead to fans supporting each other, trading tips, or even meeting up. That deep connection can help you stand out from creators who only push out content without engaging in two-way communication.

13. **Trying Different Channels for Communication**
    Even if you have a main platform, it might help to have secondary channels to reach different segments of your audience. For example, if you are a motivational speaker with a big presence on video sites, you could also start an email newsletter for those who prefer reading. Or if you usually post on a major social platform, you might create a small group chat or forum for your most dedicated fans.

Testing different channels can reveal where your strongest audience interactions happen. You might find that your short, snappy updates work best on one site, while your longer behind-the-scenes stories do better in a blog. Adapting your content to each channel's style can broaden your reach without diluting your main message.

14. **Setting Goals for Audience Growth**
    Your ultimate aim is to build recognition, but you need steps along the way. Maybe you set a goal to gain 500 new followers who match your desired profile by the end of the month. Or you aim to have 50 active participants in a live Q&A. These smaller milestones keep you motivated and let you measure progress. If you do not hit a milestone, you can revisit your tactics and adjust.

Be realistic. Rapid growth can happen, but it is not guaranteed. A slow and steady climb often results in a more loyal base. Celebrate small wins—like seeing that a particular post drew a bigger slice of your target group—because that means you are learning what works. Then, keep refining your approach for the next phase.

---

15. **Using Analytics Wisely**
    Most online platforms provide data about your followers—like where they live, when they are active, and which posts they interact with the most. Use this data to confirm or adjust your assumptions. If you thought your audience was mostly in one area, but you see a big chunk in another, you might decide to shift some content times to match that time zone. If a certain topic always gets more likes and comments, maybe that subject is a sweet spot worth exploring more.

However, avoid getting lost in the numbers. Data is a tool, not the final word on everything. Some important elements, like personal stories or emotional responses, may not show up as easily in raw stats. Use analytics to guide your strategy, but trust your own intuition and the direct feedback you get from fans.

---

16. **Avoiding Quick Fixes Like Buying Followers**
    Some creators are tempted to buy followers or use automated services to inflate their numbers quickly. This may look good at a glance, but those followers are often fake or uninterested accounts. They will not engage with your content or support you in the long run. Platforms may also penalize such actions, and real fans might question why your follower count is high but your likes or comments are low.

It is better to have a smaller, genuine group who truly care about your work than a big crowd of empty accounts. A loyal fan is worth far more than a hundred fake profiles. Real engagement, even if modest, can grow steadily over time and help you build a strong reputation among those who actually matter to you.

17. **Creating a Clear Path for Audience Members to Follow You**
    When someone discovers you, how do they stay connected? If you post a video or do a local show, make sure you provide a simple way for fans to keep track of your future updates. That might be a link to your main social page, a quick mention of your online handle, or a sign-up sheet for your newsletter at a live event. If there is no clear next step, people might lose interest and forget about you.

For instance, if you are a comedian at a small club, you could have a QR code on a small card that leads directly to your channel. If you run a workshop, end it by sharing the link to your group. Make it as easy as possible for people to follow you or join your community. Each new follower is a potential supporter who might invite their friends next time.

18. **Adjusting Over Time as Your Audience Evolves**
    Your audience might shift as you grow. Maybe you started off appealing to teenagers, but over time, your topics have matured, and you see more interest from young adults in the workforce. Or maybe your early fans loved your acoustic style, but you have switched to electronic music, attracting a different crowd. Pay attention to these changes.

If you sense a new group forming around you, you can gradually adapt your messaging or content to suit them, while still caring for your original supporters. This shift should not be abrupt, because it can leave your longtime fans confused or upset. Communicate openly if you are changing direction. Explain why, and invite them to come along, but also welcome the new folks with open arms.

19. **Planning Collaborations That Expand Your Reach**
    Collaborations can be powerful for reaching new sets of viewers or

readers who share your interests. Look for creators who have a compatible, but not identical, style or field. For example, a fitness instructor could team up with a healthy cooking expert to do a joint video on easy meals that fuel workouts. Each collaborator introduces the other to their fans, possibly bringing in fresh eyes who fit your target group.

When planning a collaboration, talk about the shared goals—like wanting to offer practical tips to busy office workers. Decide how you will present it (video, blog post, podcast) and who will handle which tasks. Make sure you both promote the project so that neither side feels all the work is on them. This can lead to a lasting relationship that benefits both audiences.

---

20. **Evaluating Offline Opportunities**
    While the internet is crucial, do not forget offline chances if they make sense for your audience. If your group is mostly local families, maybe you can sponsor a small event at the community center or set up a table at a local fair. If your group is young professionals, you might appear at a networking meetup or a conference. Real-life interactions can be memorable, and people often enjoy meeting a creator face to face.

These offline events can also be a chance to hand out flyers or small tokens that remind people of your name. Sometimes, a friendly conversation in person can create a stronger bond than a quick online exchange, especially for local audiences. Then, those people might find you online afterward and become consistent supporters.

---

21. **Speaking Directly to Your Audience in Your Work**
    In your material—whether it is a song lyric, a stand-up routine, or an online article—try speaking directly to the group you care about. For example, if you know your listeners are new parents, you could mention daily challenges they face and then offer a comedic twist or a hopeful viewpoint. If your main crowd is young professionals, you might reference office life or daily commutes. This helps them feel seen and understood, and they might think, "This person really gets me."

This does not mean you can never break from that style, but keep in mind that these references can help your core audience bond with you more deeply. Over time, they trust that your material will speak to them, because you consistently show awareness of their world.

---

22. **Avoiding Overstretching Yourself**
    When you try to appeal to everyone, you can end up overworked and scattered. You might produce content for multiple platforms that do not really align with your main audience. Or you might spend money on promotions that reach large numbers but yield little genuine engagement. This can drain your resources, both financial and emotional.

Keeping your efforts focused on a few effective channels and a clearly defined audience usually brings better results than spreading yourself too thin. If you see an area where you are getting little return, consider whether it is worth continuing there. It might be better to focus on the areas that truly bring you closer to the people you want to reach.

---

23. **Staying Flexible as You Grow**
    Finding your audience is not a one-time task. It is an ongoing process that requires adjustments. You may try a campaign that does not work well. That is okay—learn from it and move on. You may discover a completely new audience you never anticipated, like older fans who like your motivational talks, even though you originally aimed at younger listeners. Remain open and adapt your strategy to welcome them.

Being flexible also means you do not have to say "no" to everyone outside your target group. If a new group shows genuine interest, you can build a secondary branch of your audience. The key is to keep your main identity strong, so you do not lose yourself or water down your central message.

---

24. **Turning Audience Members into Ambassadors**
    When your target group connects deeply with you, some will become more than just casual fans—they will become ambassadors for your work.

They might recommend you to their friends, share your videos far and wide, or request your music on local radio stations. These enthusiastic supporters can accelerate your rise to recognition, because they do much of the word-of-mouth promotion for you.

To help this happen, show appreciation for your loyal supporters. Sometimes, a simple thank-you message or a shout-out in a live stream can mean a lot. If someone posts about you on social media, interact with it. If your budget allows, you might offer small rewards or hold raffles for your biggest fans. By treating them as partners in your success, you encourage them to keep spreading the word.

Wrapping Up Chapter 12
Reaching the right audience is about more than just amassing numbers. It is about connecting with people who genuinely care about what you do. Start by examining who already follows you, study the fans of similar creators, and think beyond basic demographics to tap into real interests and needs. Then, match your style, platforms, and messaging to the group that will resonate with your work. Gather feedback, adjust your approach, and focus on building a community that feels valued and excited to support you.

As you refine your connection with this core group, you will find that doors open more easily. Your fans will share your content with like-minded people, press outlets may notice your growing impact, and events might invite you because they see you have a loyal base. Step by step, this audience can carry you toward greater fame. In the next chapters, we will explore topics like building a strong mindset, handling stress, and avoiding mistakes that could harm your progress. By merging a clear focus on the right audience with these upcoming insights, you can keep moving forward without losing your sense of purpose.

CHAPTER 13: BUILDING A STRONG MINDSET

A strong mindset is what helps you stay confident, focused, and steady in the face of challenges. You might have the best skills in the world, but if you lose hope whenever a problem arises, you will not reach the recognition you want. This chapter will look at ways to strengthen your thoughts and attitudes so you can keep pushing forward with purpose, no matter what life throws at you.

---

1. **What Is a Strong Mindset?**
   A strong mindset is a steady way of thinking that supports your goals rather than fights them. Instead of panicking at each bump in the road, a strong thinker looks for lessons or ways around the problem. Instead of letting doubt win, they remember the times they have learned or made progress. A strong mindset does not mean you never feel sad or upset—it just means you do not let those feelings control your actions for long.

When your mindset is strong, you trust your ability to adapt. You might say, "Things are tough, but I can handle this, or at least try my best." You keep your thoughts clear so you can decide what to do next. This calm and steady attitude helps a lot if you want to become well-known in any field, because there will always be critics, setbacks, or moments when it seems progress is slow.

---

2. **Recognizing Harmful Thinking Patterns**
   Before you can grow a strong mindset, you need to see if you have any harmful thinking habits. Some common ones are:
- **All-or-nothing thoughts**: Telling yourself that you are either a complete success or a complete failure. Real life is rarely so black and white.
- **Overgeneralizing**: Taking one bad event—like a single poor review—and deciding that it means everything is bad.
- **Jumping to conclusions**: Thinking you know what others think without real proof. For example, you might assume everyone thinks you are silly because one person laughed at your idea.
- **Focusing on the negative**: Ignoring praise or good results, while giving all your attention to small mistakes or unkind comments.

If you catch yourself in these patterns, remind yourself there is a bigger picture. Try to notice positive events, too, or remember that a single mishap does not wipe out all your good work.

---

3. **Being Realistic, Not Pessimistic**
   Some people think having a strong mindset means ignoring problems or pretending everything is fine. That is not accurate. You can admit that something is difficult while still believing you can handle it. Being realistic means you look at the facts: you see that a challenge is real, but you also see that challenges can be worked through.

For example, imagine you have a big show but feel underprepared. A weak mindset might say, "I am doomed, there is no point in trying." A strong, realistic mindset might say, "I feel worried, and I might not be at my best, but I will practice extra now and do the best I can." You face the truth (you are not fully prepared), but you also trust yourself to take steps that can improve the outcome.

---

4. **Setting Personal Rules for Growth**
   Having guidelines in your mind can keep you focused. For instance, you can set a rule like, "Whenever I fail at something, I will find at least one reason why it happened, and think of one improvement to make next time." Or, "Whenever I get upset about a negative comment, I will look at three positive comments I received recently."

These small rules act like anchors. They remind you to respond in a strong way, instead of reacting out of fear or anger. Over time, following such rules becomes second nature. You begin to see setbacks not as signs that you are failing but as cues to learn something new.

---

5. **Understanding the Power of Self-Talk**
   Self-talk is the voice in your head that comments on what you are doing or feeling. It can be helpful or harmful. For instance, if you stumble during

a speech, do you think, "I messed up, I am hopeless," or "That was a slip, but I can keep going"? One leads to panic, the other leads to recovery.

Try to be kind but honest in your self-talk. If you truly made an error, do not sugarcoat it, but do not call yourself worthless. Instead, think, "I need to fix that mistake. Let's figure out how." By guiding your thoughts toward action, you keep your mindset productive.

---

6. **Turning Problems into Steps for Growth**

    A strong mindset does not see problems as the end of the road. It sees them as steps you walk over. If you face an unexpected bill for your project, you can think, "I am doomed," or you can think, "How can I earn, save, or partner with someone to handle this cost?" If your event is canceled, can you find a different venue, or move it online, or use the extra time to practice?

This idea connects with the concept of being "solution-focused." When you face a roadblock, your first question is, "What can be done?" rather than, "Why me?" The "why me?" mindset gets you stuck in feeling sorry for yourself, while "What can be done?" moves you to look for options.

---

7. **Using Visualization for Confidence**

    Visualization can help you get your mind in the right place. Close your eyes and picture yourself doing well at the task ahead—maybe you see yourself on stage, speaking or performing calmly, or you see your art being received warmly by the crowd. Imagine yourself handling nerves but staying steady.

By running this "mental video," you prepare your brain for the real thing. It is not magic; you still need to practice and be prepared. But visualization can lessen your fear and remind you that doing well is possible. Many athletes, performers, and public figures rely on such mental exercises to sharpen their mindset before big moments.

---

8. **Spending Time with Positive Influences**
   Your mindset can be shaped by the people around you. If you are always with folks who complain, show envy, or predict doom, their negativity can seep into your thoughts. If you hang out with those who see the good side, who support your growth, and who handle their own problems with grace, you might start acting the same way.

This does not mean you have to avoid everyone who ever has a bad day. But try to notice if certain relationships leave you feeling drained or hopeless. Balance those relationships by finding mentors, friends, or even online groups that encourage a strong, steady mindset. Reading or hearing uplifting stories can also play a role. Over time, you will see that it is much easier to build a strong mindset when others around you share that outlook.

---

9. **Taking Charge of Your Environment**
   Apart from people, your environment can include the media you consume, your workspace, or the habits you keep. If your room or studio is always messy, you might feel stressed before you even start working. If you watch or read things that constantly promote fear or anger, you might struggle to stay calm in your own life.

Try to tidy the space where you train or create. Have items that remind you of your goals—like a simple poster or a photo of something that gives you a sense of purpose. Consider limiting the time you spend on negative news or online arguments. This is not about ignoring real issues, but about making sure your mind is not overloaded with upset feelings that could wear you down. In a calmer environment, it is easier to keep thoughts strong and focused.

---

10. **Building Habits for Ongoing Growth**
    A strong mindset does not happen in a single day. It forms as you repeat helpful actions. You could set a routine like doing a bit of exercise or stretching each morning to clear your mind. Or you might spend 10 minutes each night writing in a notebook about the day's small successes. These habits keep your brain used to seeing positives and possibilities.

Even small routines—like taking a short walk when you feel stuck or doing a breathing exercise before bed—can boost your mental steadiness. The key is consistency. Each time you do the habit, you strengthen the mental pathways that say, "I can handle challenges by returning to calm, constructive actions."

---

11. **Learning to Set Boundaries**
    Strong-minded people also know when to say "no." If you have too many requests piling up or too many projects at once, you risk spreading yourself thin. This can lead to stress, errors, or burnout. Part of a strong mindset is recognizing that you have limits. Saying "no" to extra tasks that do not help your main goal is not selfish—sometimes, it is the best way to stay solid and deliver quality in what you do.

Boundaries also apply to situations where people treat you poorly. If someone constantly belittles your efforts, a strong mindset might prompt you to limit their influence in your life, or at least speak up about how their words make you feel. By protecting your mental space, you keep your focus on growth rather than on defending yourself against unhelpful negativity.

---

12. **Welcoming Constructive Criticism**
    Strong-minded people do not fall apart when they hear critique. They are able to separate rude or pointless insults from true, helpful feedback. If someone says, "You need to slow down when you speak on stage," a strong mind hears that and thinks, "Let me test that advice. Maybe it can help me improve." But if someone just says, "You are terrible," that same strong mind shrugs it off as unhelpful.

One way to handle critique is to say, "Thank you for pointing that out. Can you tell me more specifically what you noticed?" This invites more detail so you can decide whether the advice is valid. By responding politely, you also show that you are open to learning, which can make even the critic speak in a friendlier tone.

---

13. **Being Gentle with Yourself**
    You might see examples of strong-minded people who never seem to rest, but constantly pushing yourself can break your spirit. True strength includes knowing when to take a break. Resting is not laziness; it is part of a balanced approach. If you are tired, a short pause or a day off might refresh your brain so you come back with new focus.

Being gentle also means forgiving yourself for slips. If you lose your temper or miss a deadline, a healthy mind does not dwell forever on guilt. It admits the mistake, looks at how to avoid it next time, and moves on. Self-forgiveness frees your energy for better actions, rather than locking it away in regret.

---

14. **Handling Self-Doubt with Logic**
    Even strong-minded people feel doubt. The difference is they question those doubtful thoughts instead of accepting them as facts. If you think, "I will never make it because I messed up once," challenge that idea: "Is that truly logical? Many people have failed once and still made it. This slip might just be part of my learning."

By answering negative thoughts with logic, you protect yourself from falling into defeat. Ask yourself: "What evidence do I have that I can succeed?" List the skills and wins you have had. Doubt tends to leave out the good facts, so bring those back into the picture and see if your worries still hold. Often, you will see that your fear is bigger in your head than it is in reality.

---

15. **Focusing on Small Goals Instead of Overthinking**
    Sometimes, your mind might race with big questions like, "Will I ever be famous? Will I ever be able to stand out?" These huge thoughts can freeze you, because they are hard to answer right now. Instead, aim your mind at smaller tasks you can do today or this week. For instance, "I will practice my lines for one hour," or "I will pitch my idea to two local sponsors."

Small actions you complete will give you a sense of control and progress. Each finished step builds belief in your ability to keep moving. This approach reduces overwhelm. Rather than letting your mind spiral into fears of the future, you stay grounded in tasks that help you grow daily. Over time, these little victories add up to bigger milestones.

---

16. **Building Patience for the Long Haul**
    Recognition can take time. A strong mindset includes patience—understanding that you will not see results overnight. People who jump from one plan to another too quickly often do not stick with anything long enough to see true results. The mind that stays steady through quiet periods or slow progress is the one that eventually reaches a solid breakthrough.

Patience also means avoiding comparisons to others who might be moving faster. Their path is theirs; yours is yours. Sometimes, the fastest routes lead to flimsy success that fades quickly. True growth, built on learning and steadiness, can last longer. If you trust that each step is leading somewhere, you can handle the wait without panic.

---

17. **Learning to Adapt When Plans Change**
    No matter how carefully you plan, life can throw in surprises—a change in venue, a missed flight, a sudden expense, or a health issue. A strong-minded person does not collapse in shock; they shift gears. If the show is canceled, they might schedule a live stream at the same time to keep momentum. If a partner drops out, they look for a new partner or try to cover the gap themselves.

Adaptability is a key trait of a strong thinker. It says, "Even if something is different from what I expected, I can still find a way to move forward." This flexible approach helps you stay calm during chaos. You do not waste time blaming outside factors but instead refocus on what can be done now.

---

18. **Rewarding Progress in a Healthy Way**
    It is good to notice your wins and allow yourself to feel proud of them. That does not mean boasting or bragging. A simple internal or small outward recognition—"I did well today, and I am happy about it"—can

keep you motivated. You might also do something nice for yourself after reaching a mini-goal, like enjoying a favorite hobby for an hour.

The point is to acknowledge that your efforts paid off, which encourages your mind to keep going. However, be careful not to slip into showing off or becoming complacent. A strong mindset balances pride in what you have done with an understanding that there is more to learn. This balance keeps you both motivated and humble.

---

19. **Accepting That Some Things Are Out of Your Control**
    Part of having a strong mind is knowing where your power ends. You cannot control the weather, or whether a certain judge or influencer will like you, or whether a platform's algorithm will favor your video. Worrying about these things saps your energy. A better approach is to focus on what you can control—your skill level, your behavior, your choices.

When something outside your control affects you, the strong-minded action is to adapt, not to sink into despair. If rain cancels an outdoor event, can you move it indoors or reschedule? If an influencer ignores your emails, can you find another way to reach your intended audience? By keeping your attention on what you can change, you avoid the helpless feeling that comes from obsessing over things beyond your reach.

---

20. **Planning for Possible Setbacks**
    A strong mindset does not just react to problems—it plans for the chance that problems may happen. For example, if you are hosting a live show, you might have a backup location in mind. If you are relying on digital tools, you might have a spare device or a way to run the event offline if needed. This forward thinking can save you from panic when setbacks pop up.

You do not have to plan for every unlikely disaster, but thinking through a few "What if" scenarios can give you confidence. You feel prepared rather than anxious, because you have mapped out possible solutions. This readiness is part of mental strength—it keeps your mind from crumbling in a crisis, because you know you have options.

21. **Honoring Others' Success Rather Than Feeling Threatened**

When you see someone doing well in your field, you might feel envy. A weak mindset might say, "They are stealing my spotlight." A strong mindset says, "Good for them. Their success does not take away from my path. Maybe I can learn something from how they do things."

Showing support for others can also lead to collaborations or friendships. If you shut people out or gossip about them because you feel insecure, you lose the chance to build relationships that might help you in the future. Honoring others' achievements with a genuine smile can boost your own confidence, because it reminds you that success is possible for many, including you.

---

22. **Staying True to Your Values**
    A strong mindset is linked to your personal values. If you stand for honesty, you do not suddenly switch to shady tactics just to get ahead. If you want to be known for kindness, you do not treat people poorly when under pressure. Sticking to your values even when it is tough protects your self-respect. It also builds trust with others, because they see you are not just chasing fame at any cost.

When you face choices, ask, "Does this action fit my principles?" If it does not, your mind might feel uneasy, which can weaken your sense of self. By choosing the path that matches your values, you keep a clear conscience and a solid inner core. That sense of inner rightness is a big part of mental strength.

---

23. **Reminding Yourself Why You Started**
    During low points, recall your reason for wanting recognition or success. Was it a love of your craft? A desire to share a message? A wish to inspire others? When setbacks pile up, that original spark can get buried under stress or doubt. But if you bring it back to mind, it can refresh your drive.

You could keep a small note about your purpose where you can see it: something like, "I make music to bring people hope," or "I speak up because I believe new ideas can improve lives." Each time you read it, you reconnect with the deeper reason for your efforts. This goes beyond short-term rewards or praise. It links to what truly matters to you, feeding your determination in a more meaningful way.

---

24. **Putting It All Together for Steady Growth**
    A strong mindset is not just a collection of random tips; it is a way of life. You handle problems by looking for solutions. You speak kindly to yourself. You notice progress and correct mistakes without punishing yourself. You adapt when plans change. You honor your values even under stress. Over time, these habits build the solid mental ground you need to handle both ups and downs on your path to becoming well-known.

By developing these mental skills, you will be better prepared for the challenges that come when more eyes are on you. Critics cannot shake you as easily, and setbacks will not break your focus. In the next chapter, we will look more closely at handling stress—something every rising performer, athlete, artist, or public figure must face. There, we will explore how to keep your body and mind balanced so you do not burn out before you reach your goals.

CHAPTER 14: HANDLING STRESS

Stress is common when you are aiming for recognition. You might feel tense about upcoming performances, money, deadlines, or people's opinions. If you do not manage that stress, it can affect your health, your mood, and your work. In this chapter, we will discuss ways to handle stress in a balanced manner, so it does not drag you down but instead keeps you alert without overwhelming you.

1. **What Causes Stress?**
   Stress often happens when you think a situation is too big or too difficult for you. Your body reacts by releasing hormones like adrenaline, speeding up your heart rate, and making you feel on edge. Stress can come from many places:
- **Work overload**: Too many tasks at once, not enough time.
- **High expectations**: Feeling you must be perfect or that everyone is watching.
- **Money concerns**: Worry about bills, funding, or investments in your craft.
- **Conflict**: Arguments with people you rely on or personal issues that spill over into your professional life.
- **Sudden changes**: Last-minute schedule shifts, unexpected problems, or crises at home.

Even good events, like a big concert or an award nomination, can bring stress because of the pressure to perform well. The key is to see stress signals early and take healthy steps to handle them.

2. **Knowing Your Stress Signals**
   Your mind and body give warnings when stress is building up. You might notice:
- **Tense muscles**, especially in your shoulders or neck.
- **Faster heartbeat** or upset stomach.
- **Trouble sleeping** or waking up feeling tired.
- **Quick mood swings**—like suddenly feeling angry or tearful over small things.
- **Headaches** that come on when you are worried.

Some people withdraw from friends, others overeat or do not eat enough, and some get stuck in unproductive behaviors. By noticing these signals, you can act before stress becomes too big to handle easily.

3. **Breathing Exercises for Quick Relief**
   When you feel stress rising, one simple trick is to focus on your breathing. Take a slow, deep breath in through your nose for a count of four, hold for a second, then slowly exhale through your mouth for a count of four. Repeat several times. This can calm your nervous system and send a signal to your brain that you are not in immediate danger.

Deep breathing might seem too simple, but it can have a real effect on stress levels. If you need extra help, you can close your eyes, place a hand on your stomach, and feel it move in and out. Focusing on this rhythm pulls your mind away from panic and into a calmer state, at least for a few moments, which can be enough to plan your next step.

4. **Organizing Tasks to Avoid Overload**
   Many people get stressed because they are juggling too much and do not know what to do first. Try writing down all your tasks, then decide which ones matter most and which can wait. If you have a big project, break it into smaller actions. Then pick one action to do today, another for tomorrow, and so on.

By sorting tasks this way, you reduce the feeling of chaos. You see a clear list instead of a swirl of worries in your head. Each time you check off a task, you feel a bit lighter. This also helps you spot if you have taken on more work than you can handle. If so, you might need to say "no" to new tasks or delegate some of them to someone else.

5. **Setting Realistic Time Frames**
   Deadlines can cause stress when they are too tight. If you promise to deliver a full show or complete a big painting in half the time you actually

need, you will feel constant pressure. Try to estimate how long tasks truly take, then add some extra space in case of small delays or errors.

If you sense that your schedule is unrealistic, speak up. Maybe you can ask for an extension or break the project into phases. It is better to be honest about needing more time than to push yourself into a meltdown trying to meet an impossible deadline. A calmer work pace often results in better quality and better health in the long run.

---

6. **Saying "No" When Needed**
   We mentioned this in the previous chapter about mindset, but it is worth repeating for stress management. Too many tasks create stress. If you always say "yes" to everything—like extra gigs, side projects, or requests from friends—you might stretch yourself too thin. Learn to kindly but firmly say "no" if taking on more will harm your mental balance or the quality of your main work.

You might feel guilty turning people down, but remember that protecting your energy lets you give your best to the tasks you have already accepted. That is better than doing a sloppy job because you are exhausted. People who truly respect you will understand that you have limits.

---

7. **Staying Physically Active**
   Physical movement can help burn off stress hormones and clear your head. You do not need to do extreme workouts unless that suits your style. Even a moderate activity like walking, cycling, or dancing can help. Try to find something that you enjoy so it does not feel like a chore.

If you can spare 20-30 minutes a few times a week, that is often enough to see some positive effect on stress. Your mood might lift, and you might sleep better. Also, a brief stretch or walk before a big performance or task can release tension. It might sound too simple, but it really works for many people.

8. **Eating and Sleeping Well**
   Stress can make you forget to eat properly or keep you awake at night. Then poor nutrition and lack of sleep make you more prone to anxiety, creating a cycle. Try to keep a balanced diet—fruits, vegetables, proteins, and enough water. Avoid too many sugary snacks or huge amounts of caffeine, which can spike your energy and then drop it fast.

Aim for 7-8 hours of rest if possible. This might be hard if you have a busy schedule, but proper sleep is a key part of recovering from each day's stress. If you find it hard to fall asleep, try winding down with calm music or a simple nighttime routine. Avoid checking upsetting news or social feeds right before bed, as that can keep your mind racing.

---

9. **Finding a Reliable Friend or Mentor**
   Talking about stress with someone you trust can help lighten the load. This might be a friend, a family member, or a mentor who has walked a similar path. Sharing worries does not mean you are complaining; it can let you get an outside view. A friend might suggest simple solutions that you did not see, or they might just listen, which can be enough to make you feel better.

If you do not have a person in your immediate circle, consider looking for groups—either local or online—where people discuss similar goals or challenges. Sometimes, just knowing that others face the same stress can help you feel less alone.

---

10. **Trying Relaxation Methods**
    Relaxation does not mean you are being lazy or ignoring your tasks. It is a healthy way to recharge. Some methods include:
- **Meditation**: Sitting in a quiet spot, focusing on your breathing, and letting your thoughts settle.
- **Guided imagery**: Listening to audio tracks that guide your mind to calm scenes or peaceful ideas.
- **Light yoga**: A gentle stretch routine that combines breathing and balance, helping you loosen tight muscles.

- **Progressive muscle relaxation**: Tensing a set of muscles (like your fists, arms, shoulders) for a few seconds, then releasing. Move through different parts of your body.

Find a method that feels comfortable for you. Doing it regularly can keep stress from building to the point where it controls you.

---

11. **Making Time for Fun**
    Chasing recognition can become so consuming that you forget to do things purely for enjoyment. This can lead to constant tension. Scheduling a little fun—like playing a game, watching a humorous show, reading a light book, or playing with a pet—gives your mind a break. It lets you remember that there is more to life than work, practice, or public expectations.

Fun also fuels creativity. Sometimes, stepping away from your main goal for a short time can spark fresh ideas when you return. If you are always in "work mode," you might block the playful side of your brain that can come up with creative solutions.

---

12. **Laughing When You Can**
    Humor is a known stress-buster. Even a small laugh can lower tension and shift a sour mood. You can watch short comedic clips, read silly jokes, or share funny moments with friends. Some people also find that sharing their own embarrassing stories with close friends can turn a stressful memory into something to chuckle about. It does not solve the problem, but it gives you a mental reset.

If you are preparing for a stressful event, like a show or competition, watching or recalling something funny right before it can loosen you up. You will face the event in a lighter mood, which often helps performance.

---

13. **Staying in the Present Moment**
    Stress thrives on worries about the future or regrets about the past. One

method to reduce stress is to pull your focus onto what is happening right now. This is sometimes called "mindfulness." You might do a quick scan of your senses: "What do I hear? What do I smell? What do I feel under my feet?" This grounds you in the present.

While it might not fix every worry, it can stop your mind from spinning about 10 possible future disasters. By focusing on right now—like rehearsing this line, practicing this chord, or sending this email—you handle tasks more calmly. The future is shaped by your actions now, and letting your mind wander to worst-case scenarios only adds anxiety.

---

14. **Learning from Each Stressful Episode**
    Whenever you go through a stressful event, reflect afterwards: "What caused me the most worry? Could I have prepared differently? Did I handle it in a healthy way?" By analyzing what happened, you learn for next time. Maybe you realize you needed more rest the day before a big show, or you needed to communicate better with your team to avoid last-minute chaos.

If you handle each tough event as a learning moment, your stress-management skills keep improving. You might eventually find that the same kind of event which once terrified you now only causes mild nerves. This is because you have grown used to it and you have developed better coping strategies.

---

15. **Balancing Work and Personal Life**
    Fame-seekers can get trapped in a cycle of constantly working or thinking about their craft. This can strain relationships and remove time for personal rest. A steady schedule with set times for work, rest, and fun can help. If you share a home with family or friends, try to set clear boundaries: "I will work from these hours, then I will spend time with you," or "I need some quiet hours in the morning to practice."

By balancing these parts of life, you reduce conflict and keep your stress from spilling over into personal relationships. A stable home or social life can be a strong support system, while a chaotic one can add more stress on top of your professional load.

16. **Avoiding Relying on Unhealthy Coping**
    Some people handle stress by turning to things like too much drinking, overeating junk food, or other habits that harm their health in the long run. These might give quick relief, but they do not solve the root issue. In fact, they can create new problems (like poor health, money troubles, or addiction).

Try to replace these with healthier choices. If you catch yourself reaching for something harmful when stressed, pause and ask, "Is there another way I can calm down or feel better?" Maybe that is taking a short walk, calling a friend, or writing in a journal. Step by step, you can train your mind to pick better coping strategies.

17. **Setting Small Rewards for Hard Tasks**
    Sometimes, stress comes from doing tasks that are needed but not fun. A trick is to attach a small reward to finishing those tasks. For instance, if you have to rehearse a part of your performance you find boring, tell yourself that once you do it for 30 minutes, you can enjoy a quick break with a snack you like or watch a short video you find amusing.

This method turns a dull or tense chore into something with a light at the end of the tunnel. The reward should be modest, just enough to give you a boost, not a full day of ignoring your responsibilities. Over time, you might find that completing tasks becomes more bearable, and your stress about them is reduced.

18. **Allowing Yourself to Feel Emotions**
    Stress can sometimes increase because you think you should not feel certain emotions. You might say, "I should not feel fear," or "I should not be sad." Suppressing emotions can actually make them louder in the background. It is healthier to admit when you feel upset or anxious. Let yourself experience the emotion for a short time, maybe by writing it down or talking it through.

Then, once you have given it a voice, you can move on to problem-solving or calming methods. Denying you feel something can keep it stuck. Accepting it is the first step to letting it pass and returning to a balanced state.

---

19. **Getting Professional Help if Needed**
    If stress feels like it is out of control—leading to constant anxiety, panic attacks, or deep sadness—you may want to talk with a counselor, therapist, or doctor. There is no shame in seeking expert advice. These professionals can help you find better coping tactics, sometimes recommending group sessions or other resources.

In some cases, stress can connect with deeper issues that might need special care. By dealing with them early, you can prevent more serious effects on your health or career. Reaching for help is a sign of strength, not weakness, because it shows you take your well-being seriously.

---

20. **Keeping Perspective**
    In the race for recognition, it is easy to feel that every single event or project is a do-or-die situation. That mindset increases stress. But usually, there will be more chances, more events, more doors to open if one path fails. Keeping a wider perspective can reduce the pressure you feel. Remind yourself that your life and worth do not hang on one performance, one deal, or one interview.

If something goes wrong, you will still have other tries. By seeing the bigger picture, you help your mind stay calm. You realize that mistakes or delays are part of the process, not the end of your hopes. This perspective frees you from the burden of feeling like every moment must be perfect.

---

21. **Scheduling Breaks During Busy Periods**
    When you know a busy season is coming—like a string of concerts, back-to-back interviews, or a period of intense creation—plan small breaks in advance. You could block out an afternoon each week to do something restful, or set short quiet periods during each busy day. This

helps prevent burnout because you do not wait until you collapse to rest; you maintain your energy across the entire busy phase.

These breaks could be as simple as a walk outside, a short nap, or a peaceful cup of tea while you step away from the computer or phone. By planning them ahead, you make sure they actually happen rather than putting them off until stress has already peaked.

---

22. **Practicing Gratitude for Balance**
    One way to offset stress is to remember the good things in your life. This can be done through a short daily practice of noting a few things you are glad for: supportive friends, a skill you are proud of, a small success from the day, or simply having a place to rest. This does not make problems vanish, but it reminds you that there is more than just worry in your life.

Gratitude can shift your mood. When you notice positives, your mind relaxes a bit and sees that not everything is doom and gloom. Over time, this helps you approach stress with a calmer spirit. You still handle the problems, but you do so from a viewpoint that also sees good things around you.

---

23. **Staying True to Your Own Pace**
    In the quest for fame or recognition, it is tempting to push yourself to keep up with others who might be moving faster. This can lead to stress if your body or mind is not ready for that pace. Accept your own speed of learning or creating, and try not to compare it too harshly with someone else's. If they are doing 10 shows a month but you can only handle 5 well, then do 5 with high quality instead of 10 with panic and exhaustion.

In the end, your well-being will reflect in your work. If you are exhausted and grumpy, fans or audiences may sense that your quality is dropping. By setting a pace that allows you to stay healthy, you protect your long-term success.

---

24. **Seeing Stress as a Signal, Not an Enemy**
    Lastly, stress is not always bad. A little bit can push you to do better,

reminding you that an event is important, so you should prepare well. It becomes harmful only when it is too high and constant. Think of stress as a message from your body or mind that says, "I need attention here. Something is off." By listening to that message and acting (through rest, planning, or seeking help), you keep stress at a manageable level.

A balanced amount of stress can keep you alert and ready. It is like the excitement before performing on stage—it can sharpen your focus. The problem happens when stress builds up without relief. By using the tips from this chapter—organizing tasks, setting boundaries, finding healthy breaks, and leaning on support when needed—you can let stress help you stay motivated rather than let it break you.

Wrapping Up Chapter 14
Handling stress is about noticing the signs early, taking steps to manage your time and energy, and finding healthy ways to calm your body and mind. Everyone faces stress, but people who plan and care for themselves can keep it at a level that does not harm their progress. By pairing a strong mindset (from the previous chapter) with solid stress-handling methods, you create a stable base from which you can keep moving toward your goals.

In the next chapters, we will talk about avoiding common mistakes and learning how to adapt to new situations. Both topics will further prepare you for the unpredictable nature of seeking recognition. You will see that while missteps may happen, you can respond wisely to keep your image and your path intact. And as you continue, your growth will rest on the strength and balance you have built in your own mind and daily habits.

CHAPTER 15: AVOIDING MISTAKES

Mistakes are normal in any field, but certain ones can set you back or harm how others see you. While you should not live in fear of errors, there are ways to reduce them and handle them wisely when they happen. In this chapter, we will talk about the common mistakes people make while reaching for recognition and how to avoid or fix them. By spotting risky behavior early, you can save yourself time and trouble, keeping your path strong and respected.

---

1. **Seeing Why Mistakes Happen**
   Mistakes can stem from many sources:
- **Rushing**: When you feel pushed to do everything fast, you might skip key steps. For example, you might not proofread your writing or practice enough before a show.
- **Lack of research**: If you do not learn about your field, your audience, or best practices, you could make choices that backfire.
- **Overconfidence**: Believing you can do no wrong might keep you from double-checking your work or asking for advice, leading to errors you did not anticipate.
- **Poor planning**: If you have no clear plan or schedule, tasks can collide, and confusion can lead to mistakes like missing deadlines or forgetting important details.
- **Ignoring small signs**: Little hints that something is off—like equipment acting strange or repeated complaints—can grow into big issues if you do not address them.

Knowing these causes can help you be alert and prevent trouble before it becomes a major problem.

---

2. **Not Listening to Feedback**
   A common mistake is brushing off warnings or guidance from people who see flaws in your approach. If your coach says you need more training in certain moves, or if your editor points out weak spots in your manuscript, do not dismiss them too quickly. Some feedback might sting, but ignoring

it can lead to even bigger errors later. For instance, if you skip needed practice, you might freeze on stage, harming your reputation.

That does not mean you must follow every suggestion. Rather, weigh them with an open mind. If a tip makes sense, try it. If a comment feels off, ask a second mentor or friend for their view. By staying open to feedback, you catch and fix issues early, avoiding bigger missteps down the road.

---

3. **Overcommitting and Burning Out**
   Trying to do too many things at once can cause mistakes like forgetting lines, mixing up schedules, or delivering sloppy work. This often happens when you say "yes" to every gig, request, or partnership. While it is tempting to take all chances, quality may drop if you spread yourself too thin. Struggling to juggle everything can also lead to mental and physical exhaustion, making errors more likely.

A better plan is to pick tasks that fit your goals and focus on doing them well. If you know you can only handle a certain number of activities each month, stick to that limit. It is better to do fewer things at a high level than to do many things poorly. That way, you protect your reputation and keep your results strong.

---

4. **Not Preparing for the Unexpected**
   Things rarely go exactly as planned. You might face a sudden venue change, a tech failure, or a team member dropping out. A big mistake is acting as if nothing could ever go wrong. Then, when trouble hits, you scramble in panic. Being unprepared for the unknown can lead to rushed fixes or last-minute decisions that make matters worse.

Instead, think ahead and keep backup ideas. If you rely on a digital track for a performance, consider having an acoustic option ready in case the system fails. If you run an online event, think about what you will do if your main streaming site crashes. Having a backup does not mean being paranoid—it means being smart. You handle surprises calmly instead of letting them ruin your efforts.

---

5. **Failing to Check Sources and Facts**
   People who create content—like bloggers, speakers, or performers—might share statistics or stories to prove points. A mistake is to use information without confirming it is accurate. If you quote a number or a fact that is wrong, you might embarrass yourself later when someone points out the error. Worse, people might doubt your honesty or diligence.

Always confirm your data from reliable places, especially if you are presenting it as truth. Even if you heard it from a friend or saw it online, double-check it before repeating it in public. Doing that bit of extra research can keep your image clean and save you from having to issue apologies or corrections later.

---

6. **Ignoring Basic Politeness and Professionalism**
   It is easy to get caught up in trying to be edgy or unique, but a big mistake is dropping basic respect. Rudeness toward fans, staff, or event organizers can spread fast. A short-tempered comment caught on camera can lead to negative buzz. Or failing to reply to messages politely can make people think you are not grateful for support.

Staying professional means:

- Arriving on time or letting people know if you will be late.
- Speaking kindly and patiently, even under stress.
- Fulfilling promises you make, like sending files or paying fees.
- Treating team members or helpers with fairness, not like they are below you.

By honoring these basics, you avoid damaging your reputation through careless behavior.

---

7. **Losing Touch with Your Core Style**
   Another big mistake is trying to chase every trend or copy someone else just because they are getting attention. If you constantly change who you are to follow what is popular, you risk losing your unique value. Yes, adapting is good, but not in a way that throws away your personal style or

message. People who liked you for your original tone might feel confused if you change it abruptly.

Think carefully before shifting your brand or creative direction. Are you evolving in a real way, or are you just imitating the current craze? If you remain true to what makes you special, you hold onto the fans who appreciate your real strengths. Fads come and go, but your genuine identity can keep you standing out in the long term.

---

8. **Handling Money Poorly**
   Financial mistakes can block your rise to fame. You might overspend on fancy gear or flashy outfits you cannot afford, thinking it will pay off soon. Or you might set your prices too low because you doubt your worth, ending up without enough profit to keep going. Not keeping track of what you earn and spend can cause chaos later.

To avoid this:

- Keep a simple budget where you note all expenses and incomes.
- Plan big costs—like studio time or special equipment—when you know you can pay without risking everything else.
- If needed, get basic advice from someone who understands finances, like a friend or a professional.
- Be cautious about loans or credit cards, since debt can pile up quickly if you are not careful.

Having a steady money plan helps you keep working without constant worry. It also means you can invest wisely in things that genuinely lift your craft.

---

9. **Being Unclear About Agreements**
   Whether you are joining a team, hiring an assistant, or booking a gig, unclear agreements can cause huge mistakes later. For example, you might verbally agree on payment or responsibilities, but fail to get it in writing. If the other party disputes what was said, you have no proof. This can lead to fights or unpaid work.

Always outline key details in writing—even if it is just an email that both sides confirm. That includes payment terms, what tasks each person will handle, dates and deadlines, and how to handle issues if they arise. While it is nice to trust people, clarity prevents confusion and protects you if something goes wrong. It also shows you are professional.

10. **Not Managing Your Online Presence**
    Your online profiles and posts say a lot about you. A big mistake is ignoring how they look or what you share. If your pages are a jumble of random posts with no clear direction, new viewers might be unsure about who you are. If you post words that are too harsh or share private rants, you might chase away potential fans or business partners.

Try to keep your online spaces somewhat consistent. That does not mean being fake; it just means focusing on the image you want to present. If you have old posts that clash with your current values or might offend others unfairly, consider removing or updating them. Also, interact politely, because rude or thoughtless replies can be captured in screenshots, harming your long-term reputation.

11. **Overlooking the Power of First Impressions**
    Whether it is meeting an event host, greeting an important contact, or stepping onto a stage, first impressions matter. Some people make the mistake of acting too casual or not being ready when they first meet someone who could help their career. For example, wearing sloppy clothes to a formal setting or mumbling unprepared words in your first media interview can turn people off quickly.

Before any new meeting or event, check what the setting is like. Dress appropriately, be ready with a polite greeting, and have something brief to say about your work if asked. Being prepared does not mean being stiff. It just shows you respect the occasion and the people who took the time to meet you. This kind of care can earn you more respect and opportunities.

12. **Refusing to Learn New Skills**
    As you grow, your field might shift, or technology might change. A mistake is clinging to old methods or ignoring fresh tools because you do not like change. Suppose you are a singer who refuses to learn about online streaming even though many fans now discover music that way. You might miss out on a big audience. Or if you are a writer who does not adapt to new publishing methods, you could fall behind peers who do.

Be willing to update your skills. If you need better online marketing, consider watching tutorials or asking someone to guide you. If your craft requires new techniques, do not brush them off. Standing still while the world evolves can lead to big mistakes—namely, missing the next wave of opportunities.

---

13. **Moving Too Fast with Contracts**
    You might get excited if a manager or sponsor suddenly offers a deal, but rushing to sign a contract without reading and understanding it is a massive mistake. Some deals look sweet but have hidden terms that lock you into an unfair split of earnings, or require you to give up ownership of your work. Down the line, you could regret giving away too much control.

Always read contracts carefully. If something is confusing, ask for legal advice from a trusted lawyer or at least a knowledgeable friend. Feeling pressured to sign quickly is often a red flag. Reputable partners allow you time to consider the terms. Protecting your rights can save you from huge regrets and conflicts later.

---

14. **Not Investing in Health**
    A serious oversight is ignoring your physical or mental health while chasing attention. If you consistently skip sleep, eat poorly, or avoid exercise, you can develop health issues that stop you from performing at your best. Stress or mental strain can also escalate if you do not find ways to take breaks or talk to someone about your worries. Serious exhaustion or anxiety can lead to public meltdowns or forced cancellations.

Taking care of health is not a small thing. It affects your voice, your energy level, your creativity, and your attitude. Plan your schedule so you have rest days or small breaks. Keep an eye on your diet, and consider at least light exercise to keep your body strong. If you notice signs of depression or unmanageable stress, seek help early. Doing so helps you avoid mistakes that come from burnout or emotional outbursts.

---

15. **Neglecting Genuine Bonds**
    Focusing too heavily on your own rise can cause you to forget the people who matter—friends, family, or colleagues who were there before you gained any recognition. This can be a big mistake for two reasons: you lose a support system that keeps you grounded, and you might develop a lonely or arrogant reputation. Also, if you only connect with people for personal benefit and drop them afterward, news of such behavior can spread, hurting your image.

Stay in touch with close ones, show appreciation for their help, and be ready to support them if you can. Those real bonds can keep you steady when public life gets stressful, and they can also lead to deeper trust among people you work with. This stable social base prevents isolation and helps maintain a positive vibe around you.

---

16. **Not Paying Attention to Details**
    Small details—like the correct date, the right name spelling, the correct format—can seem minor, but ignoring them can lead to embarrassing moments. You might show up at the wrong time, send an invitation to the wrong address, or mislabel an important sponsor in a program. Such mistakes look unprofessional and can cause confusion.

Make it a habit to double-check. Before sending an email, quickly review the recipients, times, and any numbers you included. Before announcing an event, ensure all facts are accurate. Using a simple checklist for recurring tasks—like equipment setup, script reading, or meeting notes—can save you from silly slips that might harm your credibility.

---

17. **Arguing Publicly or Online**
    Sometimes, you might feel insulted by a critic or a fan who is rude,

prompting you to lash out in a public argument. But fighting openly can be a mistake because it rarely solves anything. It also can give you a bad look to bystanders. People who see you exchanging angry posts may decide you are not as professional or mature as they hoped. Instead of winning respect, you might lose it.

If you must address a negative comment, do so politely and briefly. You can say, "I understand your view, but here is my side." If the person is clearly picking a fight, it is often best to ignore them or respond offstage in private. Keeping calm in public disputes shows self-control and respect for your overall image.

---

18. **Copying Others Without Permission or Credit**
    Inspiration is one thing; stealing is another. Using someone else's words, music, or images without permission or proper credit is risky. You could face legal trouble or be labeled unoriginal. Even if you do not face legal action, fans might notice and talk about your lack of honesty. That can create a scandal that erodes trust.

If you admire another person's work, you can ask for a license or give credit if that is allowed. If you cannot get permission, create your own material. People appreciate creativity and honesty. By building on your own ideas (while learning from others ethically), you avoid the mistake of copyright breaches or plagiarism.

---

19. **Underestimating Your Audience**
    Some folks assume their viewers or listeners do not notice certain things. They might put low effort into a show, reuse old material in a lazy way, or talk down to fans. This can be a huge mistake. Audiences are often sharp and can tell when you are not giving your best. They might leave bored or insulted.

Respect your audience's time and intelligence. Prepare well, keep your quality high, and interact with them as real individuals. Show that you value their support by responding kindly to questions, offering fresh content, and being sincere. If people see you appreciate them, they are more likely to stay loyal and bring others to see your work too.

20. **Being Afraid to Admit You Are Wrong**
    When a slip happens, pretending it never happened or blaming someone else can worsen the damage. If you offend someone, share false info, or break a promise, refusing to own it might cause more people to lose trust in you. A quick, honest apology can reduce harm. You can say, "I messed up here. I am sorry. Let me correct this," and then fix what you can.

This shows humility and honesty, qualities that many fans or clients respect. It also helps you move on rather than drag out a problem. Of course, you should try to avoid the slip in the first place, but if it happens, handling it with integrity is better than denial or excuses.

---

21. **Failing to Learn from Past Errors**
    Mistakes are not all bad if you treat them as lessons. But if you keep repeating the same ones, that indicates you are not looking at what went wrong. This can stall progress. For example, if you keep scheduling too many events, leading to half-prepared shows, do not just accept it as normal. Instead, change your approach by limiting your bookings or giving yourself more lead time.

Take notes when you slip up: what caused it, how it could have been prevented, and what you will do next time. This habit can turn each error into a stepping stone. Over time, you will see fewer repeated mistakes, which leads to a smoother climb to recognition.

---

22. **Not Knowing When to Seek Help**
    Some tasks require special knowledge. Thinking you can do everything on your own—like accounting, advanced editing, or handling legal contracts—can backfire if you lack the skill. You might end up with tax problems, low-quality final products, or hidden clauses in contracts. The mistake is in not asking for assistance when needed.

That does not mean you must hire a huge team. But if there is a critical area beyond your expertise, find a trusted mentor or a professional who can guide you. Asking for help is not a sign of weakness—it is a wise choice that can keep you from big pitfalls.

23. **Expecting Overnight Success**
    It is a mistake to assume you will gain massive attention instantly or that one viral moment will solve everything. This can lead to rushing, skipping skill-building steps, or feeling crushed when the quick result does not happen. Many well-known figures built their craft and audience step by step. Waiting for a shortcut can cause you to overlook the slow but steady methods that truly matter.

Stay patient and consistent. If a lucky break comes, fine. But building a real base of supporters usually takes months or years of effort. If you chase shortcuts, you might also attract shallow fans who leave as fast as they arrived. A more stable path is likely to produce lasting respect and fewer reckless moves.

---

24. **Letting Fear of Mistakes Freeze You**
    Ironically, being so afraid of messing up can become its own mistake. If you never try new things or take healthy risks, you might not advance. Avoiding mistakes completely is impossible; you might end up stuck, missing growth chances. Part of success is stepping out of your comfort zone, knowing you might fail but can learn from it.

So, while this chapter focuses on avoiding common missteps, remember that some errors are part of learning. The real goal is to minimize needless or careless mistakes, not to avoid all action. By planning well, staying honest, listening to feedback, and protecting your health and finances, you keep the big pitfalls at bay. You then have freedom to experiment and explore your craft fully.

Wrapping Up Chapter 15
Avoiding mistakes does not mean never stumbling; it means doing your best to spot and prevent errors that can harm your progress or reputation. It involves staying professional, open-minded, prepared for the unexpected, and respectful of others. It also includes taking care of your finances, your health, and your audience's trust. If you keep these areas in check, you are less likely to face problems that could derail your climb to greater fame.

CHAPTER 16: ADJUSTING TO NEW SITUATIONS

When you are working toward recognition, you will likely face lots of changes. You might move to unfamiliar places, meet new people, or handle demands you never saw before. Even success itself can bring changes, like increased attention or new responsibilities. Knowing how to adapt lets you keep your footing. In this chapter, we will look at ways to handle fresh situations, keep calm under pressure, and grow your flexibility without losing your personal style.

1. **Why Adapting Is So Important**
   Being adaptable means you can face something unexpected and still find a way forward. In the pursuit of recognition, you might change teams, switch platforms, or shift your focus to a new niche. If you refuse to adjust, you might miss the next opportunity or fail to impress people who want something slightly different from you.

Also, the entertainment or creative world changes fast—trends come and go, technology evolves, and audience tastes shift. If you cannot bend, you risk becoming outdated. Adapting does not mean betraying your core. It means presenting your unique qualities in fresh ways that fit the current environment. Think of it like a tree that can sway in the wind but remains rooted.

2. **Reading the Room and Environment**
   The first step in adapting is awareness. When you enter a new situation—like a different city, a new event, or a new online space—pause to observe. What is the vibe? Are people relaxed and casual, or are they formal and serious? Who is in charge here, and what do they expect?

For example, if you do a talk at a business conference, you might dress more formally and focus on data or case studies. If you talk to a group of students, a looser, more fun approach might work better. By reading the room, you avoid awkward moves that clash with the setting. You can still be you, but shape your presentation in a way that connects.

3. **Keeping Your Core but Flexing the Style**
   Adjusting does not mean throwing out who you are. Rather, it is about finding the best angle for each place. Suppose you are a musician with a gentle acoustic style. If you land a show at a big festival known for louder acts, you might add stronger percussion or collaborate with a bigger band, so your sound resonates in that environment. You do not stop being an acoustic artist; you just adapt your performance to fit the larger stage.

Ask yourself, "What is the basic truth of my work?" That is your core. Then, "How can I present it here in a way that works?" That is the adapt part. This approach protects your authenticity while letting you meet various audience needs.

---

4. **Being Open to Different Cultures and Ways of Working**
   If you travel or collaborate internationally, you might face new customs or expectations. Some places expect direct communication; others value indirect hints. Some are punctual to the minute; others have a flexible sense of time. A big part of adapting is respecting these differences. If you ignore them, you might offend people or seem out of place.

Do a bit of research before going somewhere new. Ask locals or read quick guides about common practices. For example, if you are heading to a country where removing shoes before entering a studio is normal, plan for that. If you are working with a team that has a certain flow—like a brainstorming session before every meeting—join it with a friendly attitude. This makes you a good guest or partner, and they will appreciate the effort.

---

5. **Handling Sudden Popularity**
   Sometimes, a project might catch public interest faster than expected, bringing you more attention than you planned. You might get more messages, more interview requests, or more fans showing up at your events. Adjusting to this jump involves learning to manage your time and privacy carefully. You may need to set boundaries or get help from friends or an assistant to sort through inquiries.

At the same time, be careful not to become arrogant or push people away. People might want to congratulate you or simply chat. If you brush them off rudely, you risk building a bad image. Polite but firm is key. If you are too busy, say, "Thanks for reaching out, I really appreciate it. I have limited time right now, but I will do my best to respond soon." Balancing your schedule without damaging your new connections is part of adapting to a bigger platform.

6. **Adjusting to Being Unknown in a New Place**
   On the flip side, you might go somewhere new where nobody knows you. Maybe you built a name in one city or community, but in a new environment, you have to start fresh. This can feel frustrating, like you lost your advantage. But it is also a chance to refine your image and connect with new people from the ground up.

Use this as motivation. If you are unknown, you can surprise people with your skill and approach. You can also watch how local folks do things and borrow good ideas. Do not expect special treatment just because you had success elsewhere. Show respect for local norms and gradually earn respect in the new spot by being consistent, friendly, and good at what you do.

7. **Dealing with Different Age Groups**
   As your reach grows, you might face new age ranges in your audience—kids, teens, parents, older people. Adjusting your material slightly for each group can help them feel included. For instance, if you are a stand-up comedian who used to perform for college students, but now you get a family crowd, you might remove harsh language or certain jokes that do not fit a family setting.

If you aim for a wide range, find topics that connect different generations, like shared everyday experiences. If you specialize in a certain age bracket, keep your references and style targeted to them. Understanding who is in front of you at any moment helps you adapt the tone and keep everyone engaged.

8. **Using New Tools or Platforms**
   Adapting also involves learning fresh tools. Maybe an app becomes popular for sharing short clips, and your old platform is less active. If you

hold onto the old way only, you might lose momentum. Instead, explore the new app or site. It might feel odd at first, but with some practice, you can produce content that fits that environment.

Of course, do not chase every trend blindly. Pick tools that suit your craft and audience. If you are a visual artist, a picture-sharing app might make sense. If you are a speaker, a platform focusing on short videos or audio might be better. By trying out new formats, you expand your reach and show you are willing to evolve with the times.

---

9. **Changing Your Team or Network**
   As you progress, you might find yourself with a bigger team—like a manager, a publicist, or extra helpers. You might also switch teams if your goals shift. Adjusting to new people involves clear communication of what you expect and finding out how they work. If you used to do everything alone, you must learn to delegate and trust others to handle tasks.

Keep your team updated on your priorities. If there is a mismatch in styles, talk it out early rather than letting problems grow. For instance, if your manager wants you to do daily social media posts, but you prefer weekly updates, find a middle ground. Adapting to a team does not mean giving up all control—rather, it is about collaborating so your combined efforts work best.

---

10. **Facing Bigger Stages or Larger Audiences**
    Performing for a crowd of 20 is different from performing for 2,000 or 20,000. The larger the audience, the more planning and energy you need. For instance, you must learn to project your voice more, use body language that is visible from far away, and keep the crowd's attention in a bigger space. This can be intimidating at first, but with practice, it becomes easier.

Practice with a microphone or do a sound check if possible. Watch others who handle big audiences well. You may need to move around the stage more or add visuals that captivate people sitting far away. Also, be ready for bigger applause or bigger boos if the crowd is not pleased. A flexible performer can handle both extremes without losing composure.

11. **Shifting Creative Focus**

    Sometimes, you realize you want to explore a new direction. Maybe you started in comedy but feel drawn to dramatic acting. Or you used to blog about fashion, but now you want to share stories about local culture. Adjusting to a new focus can risk losing some old fans, but it might also bring new fans who love your fresh path.

To do this smoothly, explain your shift. Let your existing followers know why you are trying a different angle. Show excitement, but do not dismiss your past work as worthless. Some fans will join you in the new territory, while others might move on. That is normal. Keep producing quality in your new space, and over time, you can build a renewed audience that appreciates your direction.

---

12. **Handling Language Differences**

    If you expand to audiences who speak other languages, you might need translators, interpreters, or subtitles. Ignoring the language barrier can cause misunderstandings or limit your reach. On the other hand, showing you care about communicating well can impress people. Even learning a few basic phrases for an event in another country can warm up the audience and show respect.

Decide how far you want to go with language adaptation. If it is a short visit, hiring a translator might be enough. If you plan a long-term presence in that market, learning the language, at least at a conversational level, can pay off. This willingness to adapt can open doors and create friendships you otherwise might miss.

---

13. **Adjusting Your Budget to Fit New Levels**

    If you start earning more or gaining bigger gigs, you might be tempted to spend freely on fancy hotels, top-of-the-line gear, or lavish extras. But if your new income is not stable yet, you can quickly burn through money. On the flip side, if your budget tightens, you must adapt to cutting costs without dropping quality.

A wise approach is to watch your finances as your situation changes. If you get a temporary boost, save some of it rather than spending it all on flash. If your event funding shrinks, look for creative ways to keep the show going—maybe a smaller venue or simpler stage design. Adapting your spending to your real situation keeps you steady rather than riding a roller coaster of financial highs and lows.

14. **Learning from People More Experienced in the New Scene**
    When you move into a fresh scene—like a different region or a new genre—look for those who have been there a while. They might teach you shortcuts or common pitfalls. For example, if you are trying to break into film acting from theater, talk to someone who already made that shift. If you are stepping into children's entertainment from adult comedy, find a performer who specializes in family shows and ask about the do's and don'ts.

These mentors or guides do not have to be official teachers. They can be friends, colleagues, or local pros who share a few tips. Listening closely can save you from newbie errors. Show respect for their knowledge. Even if you have a lot of expertise in one area, be humble in the new area. That humility helps you adapt faster and gain trust.

15. **Staying Calm Under Sudden Spotlight**
    If you appear on a big TV show, get an unexpected viral post, or land a key interview, the spotlight might shine on you brighter than ever. You could face intense questions, big audiences, or critics digging into your past. Adapting means staying composed and using the chance rather than panicking.

A few tips:

- **Prepare talking points**: Know your main message so you do not freeze.
- **Breathe before responding**: Keep your pace steady when questions come fast.
- **Stay polite**: Even if faced with tough or rude questions, keep your cool.
- **Do not overshare**: Protect personal details if you do not want them out there.

This calm approach helps you sound confident and real, earning more respect from viewers.

16. **Adjusting Your Daily Routines**
    As your schedule changes, your daily life might need a new structure. If you used to have plenty of free time, but now have back-to-back events, you must plan carefully when to eat, rest, or do personal errands. Neglecting these things can lead to burnout. Adapting means creating a new routine that balances your added responsibilities with self-care.

For instance, you might switch to a shorter, more intense morning practice if you no longer have two hours each afternoon. Or you might meal-prep on weekends because weekdays became hectic. It might seem small, but these day-to-day adjustments keep you healthy and ready for the new demands of your growing career.

17. **Being Open to Feedback in New Settings**
    When you move into uncharted territory, be ready to hear fresh opinions on your work. Perhaps your old fans loved your style, but a new group wants you to refine certain aspects. This does not mean you must please everyone, but it is wise to listen. There might be genuine points that can help you improve.

Balance is key. Keep your core identity, but if many people say they cannot hear your vocals well or your comedic timing is off in this new setup, do not ignore them. Test adjustments. If they work, great. If they do not, at least you tried. This willingness to adapt based on feedback can help you win new fans and keep your older supporters engaged.

18. **Managing Emotional Shifts**
    New situations can stir big feelings—excitement, fear, or both. Adapting also means handling these emotions so they do not disrupt your performance or relationships. If you are nervous, practice some relaxation methods from earlier chapters, like deep breathing or short

mental breaks. If you are overwhelmed by success, remind yourself to stay humble and keep learning.

Talking to a friend or mentor about these feelings can help you process them. It is normal to feel unsettled when everything changes fast. Acknowledging it rather than burying it can reduce stress and let you adjust with a clearer mind.

---

19. **Handling Criticism from Old Fans**
    Sometimes, your older supporters might not like your new direction. They might say you "sold out" or forgot your roots. This can hurt, especially if they were with you from the start. The key is to talk honestly about why you made changes. Assure them you still respect your past but needed to grow or explore new ground.

It is also okay to accept that some fans will leave if they truly hate the new style. That is part of evolving. You cannot please everyone. As long as you believe in what you are doing and remain kind in your communication, you can keep moving forward without shame.

---

20. **Keeping Track of Your Growth**
    When you move around or take on new roles, it can feel like you are losing track of who you were. One way to keep perspective is to note your progress. You might keep a journal or record short audio diaries after big changes, listing what you learned, what felt strange, and how you adapted.

Reading or listening back later can remind you of how far you have come. It also helps you see patterns—maybe each time you switched environments, you faced a week of confusion before settling in. Knowing that pattern can reassure you during future shifts: "I usually feel lost for a bit, but then I find my footing."

---

21. **Trying Small Tests Before Big Leaps**
    If you are unsure about a new path, you do not have to jump in fully. You can do a small test. For example, if you want to try performing in a new

style, do a single short piece in that style instead of a full album. If you want to open a workshop in a new city, hold one small session before committing to a whole tour. These mini-steps let you gauge the response and learn about local tastes without risking too much at once.

If it goes well, you can grow from there. If it flops, you have time to adjust without a huge loss of resources or reputation. This step-by-step approach is a safe way to adapt and explore.

---

22. **Respecting Local Leaders or Gatekeepers**

    In some fields or places, there might be people who have influence, like event organizers, local media figures, or community leaders. If you arrive with a big head, ignoring those who built the scene, you might get shut out or face hostility. A better approach is to introduce yourself politely, show respect for what they have done, and ask if there is a protocol for newcomers.

This approach does not mean bowing down to unfair gatekeeping. But if you treat them rudely, you might burn bridges. By cooperating and showing you appreciate the culture or rules they uphold, you increase your chances of being welcomed. Later, once you have proven yourself, you can push for changes if needed in a calmer way.

---

23. **Using Past Experiences to Speed Up Adaptation**

    You have likely adapted before in some aspect of life—maybe moving schools, learning a new skill, or handling a shift in family life. Recall how you managed those transitions. What worked, and what did not? That personal history can guide you in future changes. For instance, if you learned you adjust better when you visit a new place ahead of time, do so again. If you found that you need a friend or partner to help you settle in, seek that support sooner.

By building on your own track record, you become a quicker, smoother adapter. You see that you have done it before and can do it again. This self-knowledge is powerful and often overlooked. Trust the strengths you developed from past challenges.

24. **Making Change Part of Your Growth**
   In the end, adjusting is not a one-time thing. As you keep climbing toward bigger recognition, new situations will appear—fresh events, new competitors, bigger budgets, changing audience tastes. If you treat each shift as an annoyance, you will tire quickly. Instead, view change as a normal aspect of growth. It is your chance to learn, refine, and discover new corners of your skill.

Staying flexible does not mean you lose who you are. It means you remain creative about how to show your identity in different worlds. By doing so, you avoid being stuck or left behind. You become a person who can thrive under many conditions, making your craft or career stronger in the long run.

Wrapping Up Chapter 16
Adjusting to new situations is about blending your true self with the needs of the moment. You watch, learn, and adapt your style or methods while keeping your core steady. Whether you are facing a bigger crowd, different language, fresh creative direction, or brand-new success, your openness to adapt will help you stay confident and relevant.

In the upcoming chapters, we will explore how to stay unique and how to balance your public work with private life. Both of these topics connect to adapting well. You want to be flexible without blending into the crowd, and you want to manage changes without forgetting your personal well-being. With these next insights, you will have even more tools to keep moving forward on your path to broader recognition while remaining true to yourself.

CHAPTER 17: STAYING UNIQUE

Standing out is often a key factor if you want to become well-known. People notice those who show something fresh or have a style that sets them apart. If you blend in too much with everyone else, it can be harder for others to remember you or feel interested in what you do. This chapter will explore how to keep a sense of uniqueness without going against who you really are. We will look at why being unique matters, how to find the special parts of your craft and personality, and how to show those parts in a thoughtful way that draws people in.

1. **Why Being Unique Counts**

When people think of famous individuals in many fields—like music, sports, art, or writing—they often recall something that sets them apart from others. It might be a certain style of singing, a bold way of dressing, a signature trick in sports, or a topic no one else tackles in writing. This uniqueness can also be a simple but strong vibe that makes an audience feel something new or unexpected.

Being unique helps people remember you. If you sound like every other singer or present yourself exactly like the rest, you risk being overlooked. Uniqueness is not about being odd for no reason—it is about finding what is special in your talent or character and letting that shine. When done honestly, it can help people connect with you, because they see something in you they do not see everywhere else.

2. **Finding Your Natural Strengths**

A big step in staying unique is noticing the qualities you already have. These might be parts of your personality, like a certain sense of humor, a calm presence, or a strong passion for certain themes. They could also be talents in your craft: maybe your drawings have a special color style, your singing voice is particularly soulful, or your speaking style is extra warm and friendly.

Think about compliments you have received in the past. Often, those hints can guide you. Maybe people always mention that your storytelling is very relatable or that your approach to dancing feels fresh. If you are not sure, ask a few friends or followers you trust, "What do you find special in my work?" You might be surprised at what they see. Once you spot these traits, you can choose to highlight them more in your public work.

---

3. **Blending Ideas from Different Places**

Sometimes, to be unique, you can combine things that others have not put together. For instance, if you are a musician who loves traditional folk tunes and modern pop beats, you could blend them into a style that feels new. If you are a writer who loves both fantasy and detective stories, you might write tales that combine magic with mystery.

This mix can create something fresh that people have not seen. It does not have to be strange—just think about what you truly like, and see if mixing them gives your work a spark. However, make sure these ideas flow well together. If two topics clash too much, you might end up with confusion rather than uniqueness. Testing different blends on a small scale (like sharing one or two short samples) can help you see what people find interesting or memorable.

---

4. **Avoiding Empty Gimmicks**

Trying to stand out does not mean you must do anything shocking or strange just to get attention. Sometimes, people might wear extreme outfits or create harsh controversy, but that approach can feel forced if it does not match who they are. Real uniqueness feels natural to the person doing it. Audiences often sense when someone is faking or using tricks only to get quick attention.

A "gimmick" might draw eyes for a short moment, but it can also push people away if it has no real meaning behind it. Instead, let your uniqueness grow from your true style. If you do like bright outfits, go for it—so long as it fits your real taste. If you are shy, you might show a softer charm that sets you apart. The key is that it feels genuine to you, so your audience trusts that it is real.

5. **Developing a Signature Style**

While "style" can mean clothing, it can also mean the way you write, the atmosphere you bring to a room, or the type of content you post online. Building a signature style involves being consistent in what you offer and how you present it, without falling into a dull routine.

For example, if you are a vlogger with a cheerful vibe and a playful approach, you might always start your videos with a quick greeting line that becomes your signature. If you are an artist who loves bright shapes, your fans might recognize your new pieces by the colors and forms you consistently use. A recognizable style can help your audience remember you instantly. However, keep room to grow over time—avoid trapping yourself in one tiny pattern that you cannot change at all.

---

6. **Being Brave with Your Choices**

Staying unique can mean taking some risks. You might worry that people will not like what makes you different. But often, showing that difference is exactly what draws your real audience closer. If you always try to please everyone, you could water down the very traits that make you memorable.

Try testing bold choices on a small scale. For instance, if you have a creative idea for a short performance, share it with a small crowd first. If the feedback is good, you can expand it. If it needs tweaks, at least you only tested it on a smaller stage. This approach lets you be brave but not reckless. Over time, as you see what works best, your confidence in showing your unique sides will grow.

---

7. **Staying Open to Inspiration While Keeping Your Core**

Being unique does not mean you do not learn from others. In fact, you might watch how other creative people stand out—maybe you notice how a dancer uses pauses in a powerful way, or how a comedian sets up unexpected punchlines. You can use those ideas to refine your own approach, but do not copy them exactly.

The line is this: learn from what impresses you, but adapt it to your own strengths. If you just replicate someone else's style, you lose what makes you you. Instead, ask, "Why does that approach work so well? How can I shape a similar method that fits my unique personality or talent?" By mixing insights from others with your own ideas, you evolve in a way that feels fresh and true.

---

8. **Being Yourself Even When You Adjust to New Scenes**

As we saw in the last chapter about adapting, you might need to alter your presentation depending on the event or the audience. However, that does not mean ditching your identity. If you are known for your calm storytelling approach, you can still keep that calm tone when performing for a new crowd—just add elements that fit the place, like a slightly different pacing or extra visuals.

Think of it like wearing different clothes for different occasions, but your face stays the same. You can be polite to fit the environment's rules, while still showing your signature humor or charm. That balance helps you remain memorable instead of blending into the background.

---

9. **Handling Copycats**

If you become known for a unique style, you might eventually see others copying bits of it. That can be frustrating, but it can also mean you inspired them. You cannot always stop copycats, but you can keep moving forward by evolving in your own authentic ways. People who follow your work closely can usually tell who the originator is and who is just mimicking.

If copying becomes blatant theft—like someone stealing your entire project or claiming credit for your artwork—you might need to speak up or use the proper channels to protect yourself. But often, it is just people seeing a trend you started and trying it themselves. Keep growing and improving; your fans will notice the real inventor behind the style.

10. Using Feedback to Strengthen Your Uniqueness

When you show your unique side, pay attention to how people react. Do they love a certain catchphrase you use or a certain visual theme you have? Do they ignore parts that you thought were brilliant? Rather than being upset if something goes unnoticed, you can learn from it. Maybe you emphasize the parts people truly connect with.

At the same time, be cautious not to bend too much. If something is precious to you but is taking time for people to appreciate, you might choose to keep doing it anyway, because it defines you. That is a choice you must make with balance: consider audience reactions, but do not let them erase the elements that you firmly believe represent your style.

---

11. Telling Your Personal Story

Often, what makes you unique goes beyond your skill. Your life experiences, values, and point of view can make your work shine in a special way. If you come from a background that shaped you, or if you overcame certain challenges, sharing that in your craft can give it depth. For instance, a singer might write lyrics reflecting personal struggles that not many people speak about. Or a filmmaker might create stories tied to the local traditions they grew up with.

When your audience sees that your art or performance comes from real events in your life, they feel a stronger link. This personal element can be something no one else can replicate, because it is about your own path and lessons. However, do not feel forced to share very private details if you are not comfortable. It is about finding the stories you do wish to show and weaving them into your public work.

---

12. Refining Over Time

Uniqueness is not a one-time "trick" you figure out and keep forever. It grows as you do. Maybe you start with a playful style of rap music. Later, you discover a serious side you want to explore in your lyrics, which changes how you sound. That new angle can become your updated unique stamp.

This process of refining is natural. You might look back at your old stuff and see it as immature or raw. That is okay. Each phase taught you something. If you see your uniqueness like a living plant, it can shift its shape and color with new experiences. Just stay clear on what you do best and what you love, so you do not lose the core that makes you stand out.

---

13. **Fighting the Urge to Fit a Mold**

Sometimes, you might feel pressure to fit into a certain mold in order to gain quick popularity. For example, if all the big hits on a music chart sound alike, you might think you should copy that sound. Or if every writer in your field uses a certain style, you might wonder if you should do the same. While learning from trends is fine, be careful about flattening your uniqueness.

Being too close to others in style might get you short-term notice, but it can also mean you are lost among the crowd. If you do step into a trend, do it in a way that still shows your identity. Maybe you adopt the general style but insert a twist that no one else does. That twist is what can set you apart and keep you from fading into the background.

---

14. **Keeping Confidence in Your Special Elements**

You might worry that your unique approach is too small or too odd for people to care about. Maybe you have a special sense of humor that is gentle instead of flashy, or you love to create smaller, detail-focused works rather than giant showy pieces. Sometimes, these quieter forms of uniqueness can still charm a loyal audience who appreciates them deeply.

Not everyone loves loud or dramatic. Some fans will welcome a thoughtful style if it is done well. Trust that your uniqueness, big or small, has worth. Stay confident, and put effort into doing it with skill. Over time, those who crave that special touch can find you and support you.

15. Mixing Professionalism with Individual Flair

When you appear in the public eye, especially for bigger opportunities, you must blend being professional with showing your personal flair. Being professional means meeting deadlines, speaking politely, and keeping your promises. Showing flair means letting your unique voice or style be seen. You do not want to be so stiff that people find you dull, nor so wild that people cannot rely on you.

For example, if you do a talk at a company event, you can still use your signature jokes or visual style—but keep within the event's guidelines (like being family-friendly if that is requested). If you are known for a certain creative twist, do not hide it just to seem "normal." Show it in a tidy way that suits the platform. That balance can impress people: they see you are reliable yet you stand out from the rest.

---

16. Being Flexible While Holding Your Spark

Sometimes, an employer, a sponsor, or a collaborator might ask you to tone down or adjust certain parts of your style to fit a project. This can be tricky. You want to be cooperative, but you also do not want to lose the spark that defines you. In these cases, talk honestly about what aspects you feel are essential and which aspects you can change.

For instance, if you are an illustrator who is asked to draw in a more realistic manner for a project, you might see if you can still keep a bit of your signature color palette. If they want you to remove it entirely, decide if you can do so without feeling false. Sometimes, adjusting is fine if you do not lose what makes you proud of your work. If it feels like the project wants to erase your identity, it might be better to pass on it.

---

17. Standing Up for Your Creative Identity

In your climb toward bigger recognition, there might be moments when you must say "no" to a chance that demands you become something you are not. This can be hard, especially if the offer promises money or exposure. Yet, if it requires you to act against your strong values or to pretend to be someone completely different, it could harm your self-respect and confuse your core fans.

Standing up for your uniqueness can mean turning down deals that compromise it too much. This does not mean refusing to grow or collaborate. It just means not letting your real self be replaced. Staying true to your core can build long-term respect. People might admire you for not bending to every push, and that can lead to better chances that match who you are.

18. Being Aware of Trends but Not Dependent on Them

Trends can be helpful if you use them wisely. For example, a trending hashtag might lead new viewers to your videos, or a certain style of reel might give you a boost in views. However, if you chase every single fad, you risk looking like you have no direction. A better approach is to pick trends that naturally fit your style. If a dance challenge is going viral and you happen to be a good dancer, it might be fun to do your own version that highlights your moves.

But do not feel forced to try every challenge if it does not match what you do. People can tell when you jump on a trend only to grab quick views without putting real heart into it. Using trends with thought and mixing in your personal flair is a smarter way to stay relevant without sacrificing your unique identity.

19. Making Friends with Other Uniquely Driven People

Finding peers who also value their own individuality can help you stay strong. You can share tips on how to maintain a special approach in a world that sometimes encourages sameness. You might collaborate and spark new ideas, or simply encourage each other when you doubt if your uniqueness matters.

Friends who appreciate uniqueness often share the belief that being different can be a strength, not a weakness. They can support you when others criticize or when you face a slow period. Having that supportive circle reminds you that forging your path is worth it, even if it takes more time or brings some risks.

20. Handling Doubt about Your Own Style

You might wake up one day thinking, "Is my approach really so great?" or "Maybe I should act more like [famous person]." That doubt is natural, especially if you see others succeeding with a style different from yours. But remember, your uniqueness gives you a special position no one else can fill exactly. If you abandon it, you might become just a copy of someone else, losing what made you stand out.

When doubt creeps in, revisit your earlier successes, read comments from fans who appreciate your unique elements, or talk to a friend who believes in your style. It is fine to tweak or grow over time, but do not throw away the essence of what makes you, you.

21. Accepting That Not Everyone Will Like Your Different Approach

Uniqueness can attract a loyal following, but it can also turn away some people who prefer more familiar approaches. That is okay. No one is liked by everyone. In fact, having a mix of strong supporters and some who do not care for you is often better than being mildly acceptable to all and not deeply loved by anyone.

If you try something bold—say, a fashion choice or a performance style—some might call it weird or over-the-top. Others might love it. Focus on the ones who appreciate it. Over time, your special brand can build a core group of fans who follow you wherever you go. That dedicated base is often more powerful than a large but lukewarm crowd.

22. Letting Your Uniqueness Shine in Many Areas

Uniqueness is not just about your product (song, art, speech). It can also show up in how you treat fans, your social media personality, or your approach to interviews. If your brand is playful, let that playfulness show when you chat with followers or post stories about your day. If your style is thoughtful and soft, reflect that in your behind-the-scenes clips or blog posts.

Being consistent across different areas helps create a fuller picture. People come to trust that you are not just putting on an act for the stage. They see your unique spark in your day-to-day behavior, too. This can strengthen your bond with those who follow you.

23. Evolving While Holding Onto Your Core Fans

As you grow and adapt, your uniqueness might change shape. Some early fans might worry that you are leaving them behind. Let them know you still value them and that you are expanding, not erasing your identity. For instance, if you change your music from purely acoustic to adding electronic elements, explain how you see it as a natural next step while keeping your emotional lyrics or certain melodic touches they love.

Handling these transitions with care can keep many old supporters while welcoming new ones. Show that your unique identity remains at the heart of your work, even if you are exploring fresh angles.

---

24. Realizing Your Uniqueness Is Ongoing

Staying unique is an ongoing process, not a one-time achievement. You may discover new parts of yourself as you try fresh techniques, meet new influences, or face different life events. Each discovery can add a new layer to your style, making it richer. The more you stay open to learning about yourself, the more genuine and evolving your uniqueness becomes.

Over time, you might become known for always having a personal stamp on whatever you do, no matter how it changes. People will be curious to see how you grow next, because they trust that you will keep bringing them something they cannot get from anyone else. That is the true power of staying unique: building a legacy that stands out over the long run.

Wrapping Up Chapter 17
Being unique is about shining a light on what makes you stand out naturally, refining it, and sharing it with the world in a way that feels right. It can involve mixing different influences, telling personal stories, or wearing a signature style that makes people think of you first. You do not need loud gimmicks or fake acts. Authentic uniqueness often wins hearts more deeply than any forced attempt at being different.

CHAPTER 18: BALANCING WORK AND HOME

Reaching for recognition can take lots of energy and time, which might strain your life at home. You could find yourself working late nights, traveling often, or feeling stressed, making it harder to focus on family, friends, or simple personal downtime. But neglecting those areas might hurt your emotional health and harm the relationships that support you. This chapter looks at ways to balance the demands of a growing public presence with the need for a stable and fulfilling personal life.

---

1. **Why Balance Is Crucial**

When you are driven to succeed, it can feel like you should focus all your effort on your craft. However, ignoring your personal life can leave you lonely, tired, or disconnected from real joy. Good moments with loved ones or time spent on yourself can reduce stress and keep you motivated. People who burn out or who lose touch with friends might feel empty, even if they achieve big public victories.

Balancing does not mean doing everything equally. Some phases of your career might need more hours than usual. But when that phase passes, you can shift some attention back to your personal circle or hobbies. The idea is to avoid letting one area become so large that it crushes the other parts of your life.

---

2. **Defining Your Priorities**

First, get clear on what truly matters to you outside of work. Maybe it is family time, a romantic relationship, friendships, or health. List them in no particular order, then think about how you can give each one enough care. If you have a partner who feels neglected, you might decide that you will reserve certain evenings just for them, even in a busy week. If your own mental health often suffers, you might plan short daily walks or quiet moments to recharge.

These priorities help you decide where to put your energy when you have a break from work. Without such clarity, free time might get wasted on aimless scrolling or doing random tasks that do not enrich your personal life. Being purposeful can help you keep the most important parts of life afloat.

3. **Building a Manageable Schedule**

A schedule that fits both your work and personal needs is central to balance. If your craft demands irregular hours, you might still find small pockets of time for personal activities. For instance, if you have a concert in the evening, you could use the late morning or early afternoon for a family lunch or a leisurely coffee chat with a friend.

Try to avoid piling up too many commitments. Look at your calendar each week or month and see where you can place personal activities. Let family members or friends know which days or hours you are free. That way, they can count on certain windows to see you or talk to you. Also, remember to set some time just for yourself—to rest or pursue a hobby. Overloading every day with tasks, even fun ones, can still cause fatigue.

4. **Communicating Honestly with Loved Ones**

Sometimes, family or friends might feel left out if you spend lots of time on your craft. The best approach is open communication. Let them know about your major events, your travel schedule, or tight deadlines. Explain why you have to focus so much during a certain period. Then, reassure them you still care about them and will spend more time together as soon as you can.

Also, listen to their concerns. If they say they rarely see you, ask how you can improve the situation. Maybe they can join you for a bit on a practice day or attend some of your performances, turning it into shared time. Or maybe you can plan a small getaway after a big project ends. Being upfront and thoughtful keeps misunderstandings from growing.

5. **Avoiding Constant Distraction**

Even when you are physically at home, your mind might be stuck on your next event or your phone might keep pinging with messages related to work. If you never switch off, your loved ones might feel you are not truly present. Try setting rules like putting your phone on silent for a certain hour each evening, or closing your laptop after a certain time.

Tell your close circle about these rules so they know you are offline or not checking emails during that period. This helps you give full attention to the people or activities around you. If an urgent matter arises, someone can reach you by a direct call, but most issues can usually wait until the next morning. Learning to unplug is a big part of real balance.

---

6. **Handling Guilt about Taking Time Off**

When you have big goals, you might feel guilty if you spend time relaxing, thinking you should always work. However, continuous work without breaks can reduce your creativity and lead to burnout. Short breaks often boost productivity because you return to tasks with a fresher mind.

Try scheduling breaks on purpose. If you see them on your calendar, you might find it easier to relax, knowing you have a set time for it. Tell yourself that rest is part of the process. Remind yourself that many successful people use breaks to stay sharp. This can reduce the feeling that time off is "wasted."

---

7. **Involving Family or Friends in Your Creative Process**

If you have a partner, children, or close pals who are curious about your craft, consider including them in simple ways. Maybe a partner can help with small backstage tasks or join you at a rehearsal if it fits. If you are a writer, ask a trusted friend to read a short draft and give feedback. Letting people see a bit of what you do can help them understand why it matters and why it can be time-consuming.

This shared experience can also become quality time, as they might enjoy learning about your work. Be sure to appreciate their involvement, though—do not push them to do tasks they dislike. A friendly request for their input is nice; forcing them to become your free staff is not. Keep it fun or meaningful, so it becomes a bonding activity rather than a chore.

8. **Saying "No" Sometimes to Protect Personal Space**

As your public presence grows, more people may invite you to events, requests, or online appearances. While these offers might be flattering, you cannot say "yes" to everything without risking your well-being. Part of balance is knowing when to decline. If you have not had family time all week, and someone invites you to another online chat, you might politely refuse or request a later date.

Turning down certain requests is not rude. It can show you are serious about keeping your life healthy and your energy high. People who truly respect you will understand. Over time, they might even admire that you have a stable personal life, which can make you more trustworthy and grounded in their eyes.

9. **Setting Boundaries on Social Media**

Social media is both a place to connect with fans and a big time-taker. Constantly scrolling or replying can eat into hours you could spend resting or talking to loved ones. If you find social media draining, consider setting limits. For example, you could spend only 30 minutes a day responding to messages or post at set times.

Also, if you post personal updates, decide how much you want to reveal about your private life. Some people share family photos or daily routines. Others keep personal matters offline. Striking a balance between connecting with fans and keeping private time truly private can help you feel secure. That way, your personal life does not become a constant public show, and you can breathe without feeling watched at all times.

10. Dealing with Travel or Long Work Hours

In fields like music tours, filming, or sports, you might be on the road often. This can strain relationships and personal routines. Before you travel, plan ahead. Schedule calls or video chats with family or close friends at times that fit both sides. Small steps like sending messages or voice notes can help maintain a sense of closeness.

If you have a partner or children, involve them by sharing stories or photos from your day. Ask about their day, too, so it is not just you talking. Also, when you return home, try to be fully present for at least a day to reconnect. If you jump right into more tasks, they might feel ignored after your absence. Balancing travel demands with genuine reconnection can keep bonds strong.

---

11. Keeping Up Personal Health

With a busy schedule, it is easy to skip workouts or eat quick, unbalanced meals. Over time, that affects your energy and mood at home. Try simple steps: walk whenever you can, pack healthy snacks instead of relying on junk food, or stretch in short breaks. If you have time for a more structured exercise routine, great—but small healthy habits also make a difference.

Mental well-being matters too. If you sense you are anxious or drained, do not ignore it. Use quick stress relief methods—like deep breathing—or talk to someone about your concerns. A healthy mind and body help you be more patient and warm at home, instead of snapping at loved ones from built-up tension.

---

12. Planning Fun Activities That Fit Your Budget and Time

Having a public life can cause financial ups and downs. Sometimes you may earn a lot from a big project, other times less. For balance, plan activities at home that do not require huge spending. A simple movie night, a homemade dinner, or a walk in a local park can be enjoyable and help you reconnect.

Grand vacations or big outings are nice if you can afford them, but they are not the only way to refresh your bonds. Consistent, small moments of fun or relaxation can be more valuable than one giant trip a year. By fitting activities into your schedule regularly, you create a steady sense of connection with friends or family.

13. Learning to Delegate Both at Work and Home

If you keep trying to manage every detail of your career plus all the chores and errands at home, you might collapse under the pressure. Delegation helps you reduce the load. At work, maybe you can hire an assistant or ask a teammate to handle certain tasks. At home, maybe your partner or kids can take on extra chores, or you can get outside help for cleaning if you can afford it.

Delegation is not about laziness; it is about using your time and energy wisely. If others around you can handle some tasks well, letting them do so can free you for things only you can do—like your craft or genuine one-on-one time with loved ones. Just remember to show appreciation to those who help you.

14. Being Flexible When Surprises Happen

Life does not always follow your perfect schedule. A child might get sick, or a last-minute work crisis might pop up. When something unexpected happens, you might have to shuffle your plans. That could mean canceling a personal event or rescheduling a work meeting. In times like these, clear communication helps.

If you must miss a family gathering because of an urgent gig, apologize sincerely and try to make it up later. If you must skip a gig because of a personal emergency, explain briefly to the event organizers. Most people understand that true emergencies can happen. Being flexible and honest can prevent a crisis in one area from completely wrecking the other.

15. Keeping Relationship Talks Respectful During Stress

Long work hours or performance stress can make you irritable. In close relationships, you might lash out or snap at small annoyances. This can damage trust over time. To avoid this mistake, notice when you feel on edge and take a small break before speaking harshly.

If an argument starts, try to remember that your loved ones are likely frustrated by your absence or your mood. Pause, breathe, and explain calmly that you are tired or stressed, and that you still value them. Working together to find a solution is better than yelling or blaming. This approach keeps your home life from crumbling under the weight of your career stress.

---

16. **Drawing the Line Between Support and Oversharing**

Somctimes, people close to you might want to help with your public image or tasks. This can be wonderful, but be aware of boundaries. If you let them read all your fan messages, for example, you might open your personal or professional life to more people than you intend. Or if you share every detail of your day online at their request, you might lose the sense of having a private zone.

Think about what you are comfortable sharing, both publicly and with close ones. You can let them help with certain tasks (like answering general emails) but keep more personal communications to yourself. This boundary protects you from feeling too exposed, which can build resentment or discomfort later.

---

17. **Revisiting Your Goals from Time to Time**

As you grow in recognition, your goals might shift. Maybe you realize you have reached a certain level of fame you are satisfied with, and you want to focus more on home life. Or maybe you still want to climb higher, which requires more sacrifices. In either case, revisit your priorities and see if your current schedule matches them.

If you find a gap—like you say family is important, but you never see them—adjust your plan. If you decide to push harder for a new milestone, let your loved ones know that you will be busier for a set period. When that period ends, remember to swing back toward more balanced time. Continually checking your path helps you avoid drifting away from what you truly want in life.

18. Celebrating Others' Achievements at Home

When you chase fame, it is easy to talk about your own projects all the time. But your loved ones might also have their own successes or daily struggles. Make sure you show interest in what they do. Ask about their day, praise them for their wins at school or work, and offer support when they face hard times.

If you live with children, show enthusiasm for their efforts in sports, music, or art. Let them see that you value their growth, not just your own. This balanced attention can strengthen family bonds, and they may be more understanding when you have to be away for a show. It is a give-and-take: you support them, and they support you.

---

19. Staying Present Even in Small Moments

Sometimes, the best connection happens in brief moments: a warm conversation over breakfast, a relaxed stroll with your friend, or a quick shared joke before bed. Do not wait for a huge vacation to show love or attention. Take advantage of these smaller daily chances to be present. Put your phone aside and really listen to what the other person says. Share your thoughts, too, but do not dominate the talk with your own news.

These small acts remind your loved ones that they are valued. When your schedule is very tight, these moments might be all you have, so make them count. A few genuine minutes of connection can hold more meaning than an hour of distracted half-listening.

---

20. Avoiding the Trap of Comparing Home Life with Others

You might see celebrities on social media posting about perfect family gatherings or luxurious trips, making you feel inadequate. Remember that social posts often show only the best parts. Everyone deals with real-life problems, but few share those openly. Focus on what works for your household and your values, not on matching an ideal image.

If you have a smaller budget or limited free time, you can still have a fulfilling home life through caring talks, simple fun, and consistent kindness. Stay true to your own path instead of trying to mirror someone else's highlight reel. This mindset helps you avoid stress or disappointment from unrealistic comparisons.

21. Learning to Pause Work at a Reasonable Time

Especially if you work from home or have no set office hours, you might slip into working until midnight every day. This can drain you and frustrate others who want to spend time with you. Try to set a stopping time whenever possible. Even if it is not the same each day, let it be known: "I will close my laptop by 9 pm tonight, so we can have some family time."

This simple boundary can give you a cut-off point. If there is unfinished business, handle it tomorrow unless it is truly urgent. Over the long run, these boundaries can protect your relationships and your health. Constantly working late can lead to feeling trapped in your own career, which is not the outcome you want.

22. Relying on a Trusted Circle for Help

If you are a parent or caretaker, balancing professional goals with home responsibilities can be extra challenging. Do not be afraid to lean on grandparents, siblings, or close friends if they are willing and able to assist. For example, if you have an important audition, a friend might babysit for an hour. If you need to travel, a sibling might check in on your pet.

Return these favors when you can. Offer to help them in some way that fits your skills or schedule. Building this support network makes your life more stable and less overwhelming. It also reminds you that you are not alone in your effort to manage both personal life and public work.

23. Creating Personal Rituals

Rituals are small repeated activities that give you a sense of comfort or connection. It could be a Sunday brunch with family, a daily bedtime story for your child, or a simple evening walk with your partner. Even if your schedule is chaotic, try to keep some rituals. They act like anchors, grounding you in everyday life no matter how famous or busy you become.

When away, you can do a shorter version of the ritual—like a quick bedtime call if you cannot read the story in person. This consistency helps loved ones feel you are still there for them in spirit, even if physically absent. It also helps you feel less disconnected from home life.

24. Valuing Home Life as Part of Your Overall Success

Finally, remember that having a stable, supportive home life can be a strong foundation for long-term success. It gives you emotional strength, a reason to keep going, and a place to relax your guard. Fame can sometimes be lonely if you do not have real friends or family to share it with. By nurturing home life, you create a personal safe space where you do not have to be "on display."

Also, fans or business partners often respect people who seem well-rounded, not those who appear chaotic and unhappy behind the scenes. Your balanced personal life might even enhance your public image as someone who is trustworthy, caring, and stable. More importantly, it keeps you happier on the inside, so your climb toward recognition does not rob you of genuine warmth and satisfaction at home.

Wrapping Up Chapter 18
Balancing work and home is about giving proper attention to the relationships and personal needs that keep you healthy and happy. It takes planning, honesty, and sometimes saying "no" to extra demands. But when you keep your personal life stable, you gain energy and peace of mind for your professional pursuits. In the chapters to come, we will explore how to handle feedback well and how to remain true to your beliefs. Both topics can help you maintain a firm stance in your growing public life, allowing you to keep your balanced life intact while you continue to rise.

CHAPTER 19: USING FEEDBACK WELL

Feedback is part of being recognized. The more people notice your work, the more they will share their opinions—some positive, some negative, and some constructive. How you handle these reactions can shape your growth and your relationships with fans, partners, and mentors. This chapter will look at ways to listen to feedback, decide which parts are useful, and apply those lessons in a balanced way. By learning to use feedback well, you can make real improvements without losing your unique voice.

1. **Why Feedback Matters**
   Feedback gives you an outside view of your work. You might feel confident about a piece of writing or a performance until someone points out a detail you missed, like unclear words or awkward pacing. Or you might feel your work is lacking something, but a supportive friend might tell you it is already strong—helping you see you are better than you think.

Feedback also shows you how your audience feels. If many people respond that a certain song resonates deeply with them, that is a clue you have found an effective style. If they say they got bored after the intro, you know you need to hook them faster. This information can guide you to refine your craft in ways that connect more strongly with your listeners or viewers.

2. **Sorting Different Types of Feedback**
   Not all feedback is the same. You will likely receive:
- **Positive feedback**: Praises and compliments.
- **Constructive feedback**: Helpful pointers on how to improve, often with examples or suggestions.
- **Negative or harsh feedback**: Critical words that might be rude or lacking in specifics.
- **Irrelevant feedback**: Comments that have nothing to do with your actual work, or that focus on personal attacks rather than content.

Your job is to figure out which feedback is valuable. Positive feedback can boost your confidence, but it is not always instructive. Constructive points are usually the most helpful. Negative comments might still hold a small truth you can learn from, but often you have to filter out insults to find it—if it is even there. Irrelevant remarks might be best ignored altogether.

3. **Responding Gracefully to Positive Comments**
   When people praise you, it can feel wonderful. However, be careful not to brush it off awkwardly or pretend you hate compliments. A kind "Thank you, that means a lot," is enough if you do not want to say more. This simple acknowledgment shows gratitude.

If you want to deepen the connection, you might ask, "Which part did you enjoy the most?" or "What was the most memorable moment for you?" This invites them to share more details, giving you clearer insight into why your work clicked. Plus, it makes them feel valued for taking the time to share their thoughts.

4. **Handling Constructive Criticism Calmly**
   Constructive criticism aims to help you improve. It might sting a little because it points out where you can do better, but try not to get defensive. Instead, thank the person for offering specific ideas. If you do not fully understand their suggestion, ask them to clarify. For example, "You mentioned my pacing is too slow—do you mean my speaking pace, or the storyline itself?"

Reflect on whether their advice aligns with your goals. If it does, see how you can apply it. Maybe you need to shorten your introduction in your next show, or maybe you need to add more dynamic transitions in your artwork. If it does not align, you can politely set it aside. The key is to stay open-minded, not let ego block useful input, and remain in control of your final decisions.

5. **Dealing with Harsh or Negative Words**
   Some comments will be plainly mean-spirited: "This is awful," or "You

have zero talent." Such remarks do not offer a path to improvement. They might be fueled by envy, anger, or simple trolling. You can:

- **Ignore them**: If it is a random online jab with no constructive detail, ignoring might be best.
- **Respond politely but briefly**: If you feel a need to address it, keep it calm. "I'm sorry you feel that way," and move on. Do not get pulled into a fight.
- **Look for any grain of truth**: Sometimes, even a rude comment might point to a genuine flaw. If you suspect that might be the case, ask yourself, "Is there anything to fix here?" If yes, fix it. If no, discard the comment.

Do not let harsh words ruin your self-esteem. Famous or not, everyone gets negativity at some point. Your mission is to stay focused on real improvements and keep your emotional balance.

---

6. **Choosing Whose Opinion to Trust**

    While you should listen to your audience, certain people in your life might have deeper knowledge or a better understanding of your goals—like a trusted mentor, coach, or colleague in your field. Their guidance can carry more weight because they have the expertise to spot specific strengths and weaknesses.

On the other hand, random strangers online might see only a fraction of your work and judge it without full context. That does not mean all their feedback is useless, but weigh it carefully. If your mentor and 50 random online users disagree, you might place more trust in the mentor's view—unless those 50 users have a clear pattern that points to a real issue.

---

7. **Asking for Specific Feedback**

    Sometimes, people want to help but do not know what kind of feedback you need. Asking specific questions guides them. For instance, if you are a writer, you might say, "Can you tell me if the opening paragraph grabs your attention?" or "Which character did you find most engaging, and why?" For a singer, "How do you feel about the tempo in the chorus—too slow, too fast, or just right?"

Specific questions help avoid vague replies like "It's good" or "It's bad." You get details you can act on. This approach also shows you are serious about improving, and people might give more thoughtful responses because you guided them on what to look for.

---

8. **When to Adapt Based on Feedback**
   If you keep hearing the same constructive point from various sources, that is a strong sign you should change something. For instance, if multiple trusted voices say your transitions between jokes feel rushed, or that your paintings lack depth in color, it is worth investigating.

Balance is key, though. If a single person comments that your comedic style is too silly, but everyone else loves it, you might decide that your silliness is part of your charm. Trends or personal tastes vary, and you cannot please everyone. The trick is to see patterns and judge whether changing aligns with your vision. When it does, try it. When it does not, stay on your path.

---

9. **Avoiding Overreaction**

Sometimes, a harsh or surprising comment can trigger a big emotional response. You might want to delete your entire project or drastically change everything. Before you do something drastic, pause. Step away from the feedback for a short time—maybe a few hours or even a day if you can. This waiting period helps you calm down, see the feedback more clearly, and make a logical decision rather than an emotional one.

Also, look at the overall feedback you have received. Often, a single negative voice can seem huge if you fixate on it, even if many others have positive or balanced opinions. Taking a broader look keeps one comment from overshadowing the rest.

---

10. **Using Feedback in Collaborative Settings**
    If you work in a team or with a partner, feedback might come through group discussions. It can be tricky because different personalities can

lead to conflicts over whose feedback is correct. Keep an open, respectful tone: "I hear your idea. Here's my concern, though—what if we try it this way?" or "That's an interesting point. Let's see how it fits our main goal."

Team environments benefit from structured feedback. You might schedule a quick round where each member shares one positive point and one improvement point. This method ensures no one hogs the floor and that each person's perspective is heard. Decide as a group how to use the suggestions. If there is major disagreement, consider testing both ideas in a small trial to see which works better.

---

11. **Turning Positive Feedback into Growth**
    Positive feedback can feel wonderful, but it is easy to dismiss it as just nice words. However, analyzing positive remarks helps you see what you do well. Maybe people mention your voice has a calming effect, or your writing is full of vivid imagery. If you notice certain strengths, consider how to build on them. Could you highlight that calmness more in a guided podcast? Could you lean more on visual scenes in your next story?

Celebrating your strong points is not arrogance. It is about knowing your assets and using them wisely. Share these strengths confidently while still working on your weaker areas.

---

12. **Keeping Self-Confidence While Growing**
    Using feedback well does not mean you consider yourself flawed or incompetent. It means you are open to leveling up your skills. Remind yourself of your achievements so far—like a successful performance or a piece that touched people's hearts. These successes prove you already have value. Feedback merely helps you refine further.

People who handle feedback gracefully often come across as more mature and professional. They do not crumble under criticism, nor do they become smug when praised. They stay balanced, recognizing that they have come a long way but can still go further.

---

13. **Knowing When to Ask for Professional Reviews**
    At some point, you might want a higher level of evaluation—like a coach, an editor, or an experienced critic. For example, a dancer might ask a respected choreographer to review a routine. A writer might hire a professional editor for a deep critique. These pro reviews can be more intense but also more valuable.

If you go for this, prepare yourself mentally. Professionals might be direct about areas that need work. Listen closely, ask questions, and consider whether their suggestions align with your goals. It is also fair to question or discuss points you do not agree with, but do so politely. Their perspective may help you skip months or years of guesswork.

---

14. **Handling Public Critiques (e.g., Reviews, News Articles)**
    As you become more visible, you might see formal reviews or articles about you in newspapers, magazines, or blogs. These can shape public perception. If a review is positive, you can share it with your audience. If it is negative, try not to lash out publicly. Instead, read it carefully. A professional reviewer usually provides reasons for their opinion. Maybe they found your storyline confusing or your performance lacking energy.

If you think they misunderstood your work, you can politely clarify in a small statement, but avoid a big feud. Sometimes, ignoring a harsh review is best, especially if it seems motivated by bias. Maintain a calm public face. Over time, consistently strong work can outweigh a few negative articles.

---

15. **Using Online Polls or Surveys**
    If you want to collect broad feedback, online polls or surveys can be useful. You can ask your followers, "Which song style do you like best?" or "Did you find the last video too long, too short, or just right?" Keep it short and straightforward so people actually respond.

Use the results with caution—some participants might just click randomly, and the poll might not represent all of your fans. But it still can give you a quick sense of preferences. Combine this data with your own artistic judgment. If a majority says they prefer your acoustic style, but you personally love your new electric sound, you might blend them in a way that satisfies both your passion and your audience's tastes.

---

16. **Knowing When to Stand Your Ground**
    Sometimes, your unique or experimental approach might not be universally welcomed. A portion of your audience—or even some mentors—may insist you revert to a safer, more traditional style. Before changing, ask yourself if this new direction feels right in your heart. If so, you may need to keep going despite lukewarm feedback. Innovation often faces initial resistance.

Balance risk with logic. If you see potential in your new style, give it time to grow. If it fails repeatedly, you might adjust. But do not kill a bold idea just because it did not get instant applause. Some legendary creators were initially misunderstood. Trust your instincts while staying open to slight modifications that might help the idea land better.

---

17. **Avoiding Confusion from Too Many Voices**
    If you ask for feedback from too many people at once—mentors, fans, relatives, random social media groups—you might get conflicting advice. That can leave you confused about which way to go. One solution is to limit the circle of people you ask for detailed critique, focusing on those who understand your goals and have some expertise or genuine interest in your field.

You can still read general comments, but weigh them against the opinions of your core group. Another strategy is to decide on a single question to ask each group. For example, your mentor might give you overall structure feedback, while your fans comment on how entertaining your new piece is. This keeps their roles clear and avoids meltdown from an overload of opinions.

---

18. **Applying Feedback in Steps**
    Implementing big changes all at once can be overwhelming. If your feedback list is long, tackle it in stages. Prioritize the points you think will

bring the biggest impact or that keep coming up repeatedly. For example, if multiple people say your vocals are drowned out by your background music, fix that first.

After you make the change, test it—perform again or show the updated version. See if the same criticism appears or if new criticisms pop up. Gradual improvement helps you manage the process without losing track of what actually made your work special in the first place.

---

19. **Practicing "Feedback Breaks"**
    If you constantly read or listen to critiques, you can become too self-conscious. It is good to step away sometimes and just create freely, remembering why you love your craft in the first place. Schedule a "no feedback" period where you do not actively seek opinions, letting yourself experiment or produce in a more private zone.

This break allows you to find your internal voice again. Afterward, you can re-enter the feedback loop with fresh eyes, merging your renewed personal intuition with outside guidance. This cycle of checking in with yourself, then with others, can keep your creativity balanced.

---

20. **Teaching Yourself to Filter Personal Attacks**
    As you grow, some feedback will not be about your work—it might attack you personally. For instance, mocking your appearance, your background, or your personality. This is not real critique about your craft. Remind yourself that such remarks do not define your skill. They might indicate the critic's own issues or biases.

Learning to separate "They criticized the structure of my story" (useful) from "They said I'm ugly or boring as a person" (not useful) can save your mental health. You can discard personal attacks as noise. They do not help you get better at your craft. If they become severe or harassing, block or report as needed. Your mental well-being matters more than engaging with trolls.

---

21. **Keeping Records of Feedback**
    If you get feedback from multiple sources over time, it can be helpful to keep notes. You might have a simple document where you list repeated comments—both good and bad. You might note the date, the source, and the main point. Over months or years, patterns may emerge. For example, you might see that "lack of clarity in lyrics" shows up frequently.

When you notice recurring themes, you can focus on fixing them. Also, seeing that you have improved on a once-common complaint can boost your confidence. Tracking feedback also helps you see that some comments come and go with trends, while others remain consistent, pointing to core issues or strengths in your work.

---

22. **Acknowledging Your Growth Publicly**
    If you implement feedback that leads to visible improvements, you can let your audience know you appreciate their input. For instance, "Many of you said the lighting in my videos was too dark, so I've adjusted it. Let me know if it's better now!" This approach shows you care about your audience's experience and that you are not above learning.

Being open about your learning process can build a stronger bond with fans. They see you as a real person who strives to get better, and it can encourage them to keep sharing insights that might help you further. Just ensure you do not come across as someone who changes direction every time a new comment appears. Show that you evaluate suggestions carefully and choose the ones that truly elevate your work.

---

23. **Balancing Feedback with Personal Vision**
    Ultimately, feedback should not override your personal vision. You started your craft for a reason—maybe a passion or a story you want to share. Keep that mission in front of you. Feedback is meant to refine or clarify that mission, not replace it with someone else's dream.

When a suggestion helps your vision shine brighter, adopt it. When it pulls you away from what you believe in, let it go. This balance ensures you remain true to yourself while still evolving. It is a delicate dance between listening and leading, but when done well, it can produce work that is both genuine and ever-improving.

---

24. **Seeing Feedback as a Tool for Continuous Improvement**
    If you treat feedback as a normal, even welcome part of your process, it becomes less scary. You realize it is just another step, like practicing or editing. Each new piece of feedback can either confirm what works or alert you to what does not. If you respond to it with calm thinking, you can keep growing throughout your entire journey.

This mindset transforms criticism from a threat into a resource. Even negative or harsh words can sometimes sharpen your perspective or challenge you to become stronger. Positive feedback can motivate you to expand on what you do best. Over time, you will develop a healthier relationship with outside opinions, seeing them as partners in your quest for excellence rather than obstacles or final judgments.

Wrapping Up Chapter 19
Using feedback well involves filtering out noise, embracing constructive points, and keeping your core vision intact. You learn to sort different types of comments and respond thoughtfully, whether they are praises, useful critiques, or mean jabs. Instead of letting feedback shake your confidence, you use it to refine your abilities. In this way, feedback becomes a vital tool that supports your ongoing progress and helps you connect more deeply with your audience.

Next, we will move to the final chapter—staying true to your beliefs. As you grow and gain recognition, you may face pressure to act in ways that conflict with your values or to promote ideas you do not support. We will discuss how to hold on to your core principles so that your public success does not erode the personal integrity at the heart of all your efforts.

CHAPTER 20: STAYING TRUE TO YOUR BELIEFS

Success can bring new influences and demands. People might want you to endorse products, take certain public positions, or do things that conflict with what you truly believe. In the rush of fame, it is easy to get caught up and forget your original principles. This final chapter will focus on how to protect your core beliefs and values even as you climb higher. When you stay true to who you are, your achievements gain lasting meaning, and you keep a sense of inner peace that no amount of public attention can replace.

1. **Why Your Beliefs Matter**
   Your beliefs—values, ethics, moral codes—are part of what define you as a person. They guide decisions on how you treat others, what you create, and how you use your influence. Abandoning them for short-term gains might bring quick rewards, but it can also lead to regret or a shaky reputation. When you stay consistent, you maintain credibility both with yourself and your supporters.

Think of your beliefs as a compass that keeps you on track. You might explore new paths and changes in style, but the compass ensures you do not wander too far from what you stand for. Without that compass, you risk becoming a product of others' demands, losing the uniqueness and sincerity that drew people to you in the first place.

2. **Identifying Your Core Principles**
   Before you can stay true, you must be clear about what you truly believe. Set aside time to list or think deeply about principles that you hold dear. For instance:
- **Honesty**: Avoiding lies or half-truths in your public communication.
- **Kindness**: Treating fans, co-workers, and strangers with respect.
- **Creativity**: Ensuring your work remains genuine, not just a copy of trends.
- **Responsibility**: Making sure you do not misuse your platform to harm or mislead.
- **Positive impact**: Maybe you want your work to uplift or educate people.

These are just examples. Your principles might be different or more specific. The key is to know them clearly so you can notice when something pushes you away from them.

3. **Facing Temptations for Quick Gains**
   As your name grows, you might be offered shortcuts—opportunities that offer money or visibility but clash with your ethics. For instance, a brand might want you to promote a product you do not trust, or a manager might suggest you exaggerate a sob story to get attention.

Ask yourself: "If I do this, how will I feel tomorrow or next year? Will I still respect myself?" If the answer is no, that is a warning sign. Sometimes, turning down such offers might mean less immediate income or publicity, but it keeps your conscience clear. In the long run, that integrity can strengthen your bond with fans who see you as authentic, leading to more stable success.

4. **Being Aware of Peer Pressure in the Industry**
   Peers or mentors might press you to follow certain paths—like adopting a more provocative style, using harsh language, or associating with controversial figures—because "that's how it's done." While advice can be helpful, do not blindly follow instructions that conflict with your values.

If a peer suggests an approach that feels off, ask questions. Why do they think it is necessary? Is there a way to meet the same goal without betraying your beliefs? Could you adapt the idea so it aligns with who you are? If none of that works, it might be time to politely decline. A little friction now is better than deep regret later.

5. **Handling Pressure to Speak on Big Issues**
   Once you are known, people might want you to comment on political or social topics, expecting you to take a stand. If you have strong beliefs about those issues, speaking up can feel natural. However, if you do not feel informed enough or do not want to get involved, you have the right to decline.

That said, if an issue directly relates to your core values—like fairness, kindness, or responsibility—and you are passionate about it, your voice might help bring positive change. Just ensure you speak from a place of knowledge, not just emotion. Research the topic so you can share a thoughtful viewpoint. Remember that once you share a public stance, people will watch how well your actions match your words.

---

6. **Communicating Boundaries to Your Team**
   If you have a manager, agent, or PR team, let them know upfront about your non-negotiable values. For instance, if you refuse to endorse certain products (like cigarettes, gambling, or something else you oppose), make that clear. If you do not want to use certain language or appear in certain ads, state it early.

Your team might push back, saying you could earn big money from such deals. But if you firmly believe it goes against your principles, insist. This helps avoid later conflicts where they sign you up for something you must cancel. A clear conversation about your moral lines keeps everyone on the same page.

---

7. **Choosing Work That Resonates with Your Values**
   You might get offers for roles, collaborations, or partnerships that do not align with your beliefs. Maybe it is an event sponsored by a group whose practices you disagree with. Or a film script that promotes harmful stereotypes. If you accept such work, you might feel uneasy or even damage your reputation among followers who share your values.

Picking projects that match your ethics ensures you present a consistent image and feel good about your involvement. This might limit your options in some cases, but it also protects you from endorsing something that leads to guilt or backlash. Over time, you can build a brand known for sincerity and responsible choices, which can attract fans who respect your stance.

---

8. **Dealing with Criticism for Sticking to Principles**
   Sometimes, fans or media might criticize you for turning down

opportunities or for publicly supporting a cause. They could say you are throwing away chances or ignoring your main work for activism. Remember that not everyone will share your priorities. Your job is to live in a way that feels right to you.

If you face criticism, calmly explain your reasoning if it seems helpful to do so. For example, "I chose not to do that show because it promoted ideas I strongly disagree with." Keep it simple—no need to attack the critics. Not everyone will accept your explanation, and that is okay. The important thing is you remain faithful to your conscience.

---

9. **Balancing Personal Beliefs with a Diverse Audience**
   Your fans may come from many backgrounds. Some might have beliefs that clash with yours. You do not have to change your morals to please them, but you can still treat them with respect. Focus on the shared interest that brought them to your work.

If they demand you compromise your values just to keep their support, consider whether you truly want fans who cannot accept your authenticity. Usually, fans appreciate honesty, even if they do not agree with all your stances. Being true to your beliefs can form a loyal following that stands by you, knowing exactly who you are.

---

10. **Avoiding Hidden Conflicts of Interest**
    As you gain fame, you might have chances to invest in businesses or partner with other brands. Be mindful of conflicts of interest. If you publicly support environmental causes but invest in a company that heavily pollutes, people will see the contradiction. That can damage trust.

Before entering partnerships, check what the other side stands for and does in practice. If it goes against your public or personal values, it might be better to pass. A hidden conflict can surface later, leading to accusations of hypocrisy that are hard to shake off. Staying consistent in both public statements and private dealings preserves your integrity over time.

11. **Staying Humble and Avoiding Pride**
    Having strong beliefs does not mean looking down on others who think differently. If you act superior or self-righteous, you risk alienating potential collaborators or fans who might otherwise respect you. Instead, hold your beliefs firmly while staying open to dialogue. You can say, "This is what I believe," without implying anyone else is lesser.

Humility also means acknowledging you can learn. If new evidence or experiences challenge a belief, be willing to examine it. Being true to your beliefs does not mean being stuck if reality shows a need to grow or adapt. It means you remain authentic in your approach to understanding the world.

---

12. **Being Consistent in Public and Private**
    Nothing destroys integrity faster than behaving one way on stage and a completely different way offstage. If you preach kindness but treat your team rudely, word will spread. If you condemn dishonesty but lie to your audience, eventually someone will reveal the truth.

Striving for consistency is not about being flawless—we all make mistakes. But do your best to align your personal life with the values you present publicly. If you slip up, own it, apologize, and correct course. Admitting errors can show maturity and help rebuild trust, but repeated hypocrisy might drive supporters away for good.

---

13. **Handling Conflicting Beliefs Within the Team**
    If your bandmates, co-authors, or collaborators hold different values, conflicts can arise. Maybe a band member wants to accept a sponsorship from a company you oppose. Or a co-writer wants to include content you find offensive. You will need calm discussions to find middle ground or realize you must part ways.

Keep communication respectful. Outline your stance: "I'm not comfortable with that sponsor because it goes against my commitment to fair trade." Listen to their reasons, too. If you cannot agree, it may mean adjusting the project or letting them proceed separately. Maintaining personal integrity sometimes requires tough decisions, even within close creative teams.

14. **Using Your Platform Responsibly**
    As your recognition grows, your words can carry extra weight. If you share harmful information or hateful messages, it can do more damage than if you were unknown. Being true to your beliefs means ensuring what you post or say publicly does not harm others contrary to your values.

For instance, if you believe in respect for all communities, avoid endorsing jokes or content that degrade certain groups. If you advocate truthfulness, check facts before reposting articles. This consistency builds credibility: people see that you do not compromise your values just for clicks or trends.

15. **Resisting the Lure of Controversy for Attention**
    Sometimes, stirring up controversy can bring a quick burst of fame, but it might run against your ethics if you are doing it just for shock value. If you truly feel strongly about an issue, addressing it honestly can be powerful. But if you create drama only to get headlines, you risk cheapening your craft and disrespecting your own moral code.

Ask yourself: "Would I still do this if no one watched?" If the answer is no, that might be a sign you are just chasing attention. True belief-based actions do not hinge on applause or coverage; they come from genuine conviction. Sticking to that conviction avoids the trap of shallow controversies that can tarnish your reputation long-term.

16. **Learning from Role Models Who Kept Their Integrity**
    Look at others in your field who are known for standing by their principles. Read interviews or watch documentaries about how they handled pressure or tempting offers. Many share stories of turning down lucrative deals or suffering temporary career setbacks, but eventually earning deeper respect.

Seeing real examples can remind you that you are not alone. It can also give you practical ideas on how to say no gracefully or how to handle criticism. Role models show that success and strong values can go hand in hand, even if the path is more challenging.

17. **Staying True Even During Setbacks**
    Sometimes, you might face low points—projects fail, money is tight, or your popularity dips. In these vulnerable times, you might be tempted to compromise your beliefs for a lifeline. Perhaps a shady sponsor appears offering quick cash, or a rumor can be exploited for attention.

Recall your long-term goals and the kind of legacy you want. Ask, "If I do this just to solve today's problem, will I regret it tomorrow?" Usually, short-term solutions that betray your values lead to bigger issues later, like guilt or lost credibility. Holding steady can be tough, but it keeps your foundation strong for future opportunities you can be proud of.

18. **Developing Self-Reflection Habits**
    To ensure you stay aligned with your principles, practice regular self-reflection. This could be journaling each week about decisions you made: "Did I handle that event in a way that reflects my honesty? Did I treat my staff kindly?" Or you might do a mental check-in after each performance or major choice.

Self-reflection helps you spot small drifts before they become major issues. If you see that you compromised without realizing it, you can take steps to correct it or do better next time. This ongoing mindfulness keeps your moral compass well-tuned.

19. **Encouraging Support from Like-Minded Communities**
    Surrounding yourself with people who share your values can give you strength. This does not mean creating an echo chamber—exposure to different views is valuable. But having at least a few close friends, mentors, or community members who appreciate your moral standpoint can offer support when you face tough choices.

They can remind you why your beliefs matter, celebrate your integrity, and stand by you if critics lash out. This supportive circle acts like a safety net, helping you stay firm and reminding you that you are not standing alone.

---

20. **Responding to Mistakes with Honesty**
    Even with the best intentions, mistakes happen. You might find yourself endorsing something that later turns out to be problematic, or you might lose your temper publicly in a way that contradicts your value of kindness. When this occurs, the key is honesty. Apologize if needed, explain what went wrong, and outline how you will fix it.

People can forgive errors if they see you truly take responsibility and learn. Cover-ups or excuses can cause a bigger scandal and deeper mistrust. By facing mistakes directly, you show that you respect your audience enough to be transparent and that you still hold your beliefs dear, despite a slip-up.

---

21. **Integrating Beliefs into Your Creative Work**
    One of the best ways to stay true is to let your convictions shine through your art or performances. If you value hope, weave messages of hope into your songs or stories. If you champion equality, highlight diverse voices or characters. Doing this not only keeps you centered on your values but also helps you attract fans who resonate with them.

Be careful not to turn every piece into a heavy sermon, unless that is your style. Subtle or symbolic touches can be just as effective. By embedding your beliefs in your craft, you create an authentic signature that sets you apart and keeps you grounded.

---

22. **Balancing Privacy and Advocacy**
    You might strongly support certain causes but prefer to keep some aspects of your personal life private. That is allowed. You do not have to bare every detail to prove you hold certain values. Pick the public actions that genuinely help the cause or express your stance—like donating to a

fundraiser, creating an awareness campaign, or simply speaking positively about an issue at an event.

At the same time, do not pressure yourself to become a full-time activist unless that is truly your calling. Balancing your creative output with occasional advocacy can be enough if you handle it sincerely. The point is to act consistently with your beliefs without feeling forced to share every personal detail or moment.

---

23. **Encouraging Younger or Newer Artists to Keep Their Values**
    As you become more established, you may meet younger or less-experienced creators who admire you. They might ask for advice on handling moral dilemmas. This is a chance to spread the idea that success does not require selling out your core. Share your own stories of times you refused certain offers, or how you dealt with peer pressure.

By guiding them, you create a culture where staying true is seen as a strength, not a limitation. This positive influence can ripple outward, leading more people in your field to hold onto their ethics. It also reinforces your own resolve to practice what you preach.

---

24. **Leaving a Legacy of Integrity**
    In the end, when people talk about your journey, they might recall your hits or awards, but they will also remember how you carried yourself. Were you reliable and sincere, or did you bend with every commercial wind? Did you use your platform to spread compassion or to sow division? Staying true to your beliefs ensures your story stands out as one of real substance.

Beyond your immediate career, that legacy can inspire others. They see that you can climb to recognition while honoring what matters. And for you personally, it brings the inner peace of knowing you never lost yourself in the process. Even if fame fades, your conscience stays intact, and that is worth more than any fleeting spotlight.

Wrapping Up Chapter 20

Holding on to your core principles is the final piece of building a lasting and meaningful presence in the public eye. It ties together everything you have learned—developing skill, building a strong mindset, handling stress, connecting with the right audience, welcoming feedback, and remaining unique. Through it all, your beliefs serve as your guiding star.

With these 20 chapters, you have a roadmap on how to hone your talents, engage audiences, handle the pressures of public attention, and still remain true to who you are. Becoming well-known can be exciting and challenging in equal measure, but if you stay grounded, keep learning, and uphold your core values, you stand a strong chance of not just being famous, but also making a genuine impact in your field and in the lives of those who follow your work.

Continue forward with courage and authenticity, knowing that each step is part of a bigger story—your own story—shaped by the skills you develop, the connections you form, and the values you protect. May your journey bring you growth, fulfillment, and the recognition that comes from presenting your real, remarkable self to the world.

www.ingramcontent.com/pod-product-compliance
Lightning Source LLC
LaVergne TN
LVHW012103070526
838202LV00056B/5608